A Walking Tour of
Historic Edenton

Edenton Woman's Club *Walking Tour of Edenton* Book Committee

Peggy Arnold, Editor
Mary Ann Climer
Beatrice Johnson
Linda Lane
Susan Nolton, President EWC 2013-15
Pam Wagner
Susan Williams, Chairperson

Book design, typesetting, and photography by Kip Shaw

Contents

Introduction

The Town of Edenton is a museum unto itself, and perhaps the best way to enjoy its beauty, history, and architecture is to walk its streets. There one can best see the details of Edenton's homes, gardens, buildings, and historic sites and feel how they relate to the beauty of the water and the landscape. On the streets the visitor can catch a glimpse of life as it is currently lived in this real historic town and experience the richness of small town life, lived in a setting of beauty and history.

In this book we outline several walking tours beginning with the "Museum Trail" which guides the walker past the town's most important historic landmarks. This tour takes one from colonial days into the early years of the new nation and highlights the homes of historic figures as well as churches, monuments, cannons, the lighthouse, the Courthouse, and Edenton's first jail.

Subsequent tours highlight the buildings and homes of the Cotton Mill, an important early twentieth century industry and a culture unto itself; other tours feature the homes of the wealthy and the humble representing a wide variety of architecture from the eighteenth to the twentieth century.

Brief descriptions and histories are included here but for more comprehensive historical and architectural information one can refer to *Edenton: An Architectural Portrait*, by Thomas R. Butchko. The text for this Walking Tour is based upon that book and an earlier Guide Book written by Elizabeth Vann Moore. The best source for information about properties in Chowan County is *Between the River and the Sound, the Architectural Heritage of Chowan County, North Carolina*, also by Thomas Butchko. All are published by The Edenton Woman's Club.

Except for the Barker House, the Cupola House, and the Iredell House, all homes are privately owned and are not open to the public. Access to private homes is offered during the Christmas Tour held yearly in early December and during the Pilgrimage Tour of Homes held near the end of April in odd numbered years.

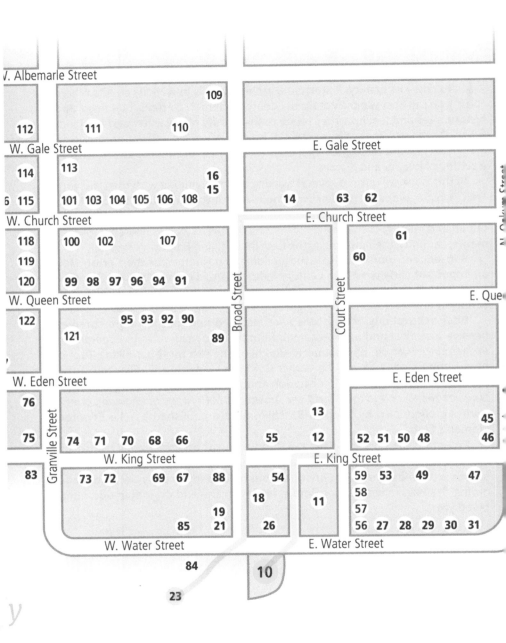

W. Albemarle Street

109

112   111   110

W. Gale Street   E. Gale Street

114   113   16
                                   15
6 115   101 103 104 105 106 108   14   63   62

W. Church Street   E. Church Street

118   100   102   107   61

119   60

120   99 98 97 96 94 91

W. Queen Street   E. Que

122   95 93 92 90

121   89

W. Eden Street   E. Eden Street

76   13   45

75   74 71 70 68 66   55   12   52 51 50 48   46

W. King Street   E. King Street

83   73 72   69 67 88   54   59 53   49   47
                                 18   58
                         19   11 57
                 85   21   26   56 27 28 29 30 31

W. Water Street   E. Water Street

84
                          10
23

Broad Street

Court Street

Granville Street

8

Museum Trail of History

Barker House
509 South Broad Street
1782
National Register of Historic Places

Penelope Barker is credited with organizing one of the earliest women's political actions in the United States. Born in 1728, she was widowed three times and outlived all five of her children. Penelope built the home with her third husband, Thomas Barker, in 1782, two blocks north of its current location.

In 1952, the Junior Chamber of Commerce, Business and Professional Women's Club, and Edenton Woman's Club raised monies to move the home to its present site and restore it for public use.

While Thomas was in England acting as the North Carolina agent, Penelope was busy at home. She was adamant in her support for the American Colonists stating, "Maybe it has only been men who have protested the king up to now. That only means we women have taken too long to let our voice be heard". She led a group of Edenton women to protest the British king's taxation by staging their own Edenton Tea Party.

On October 25, 1774, fifty-one Edenton women signed a petition saying that as women they were "determined to give memorable proof of their patriotism" and could not be "indifferent on any occasion that appears nearly to affect the peace and happiness of our country... it is a duty that we owe, not only to our near and dear connections...but to ourselves..." The petition was sent to King George.

The Penelope Barker House and Edenton Welcome Center is open from 10 am to 4 pm. For more information please call 252-482-7800 or visit their website at www.ehcnc.org.

Courthouse Green
East King Street

The Courthouse Green, public property since the town of Edenton was laid out in 1712, continues as a location for memorials, celebrations, and public events. To the north is the Historic Chowan County Courthouse; at the southern end is a large marble memorial to Edenton merchant Joseph Hewes (1730–1779), one of the three North Carolina signers of the Declaration of Independence.

To the west across Colonial Avenue, a handsome bronze teapot commemorating the Edenton Tea Party of October 25, 1774 sits on a pedestal beside the fence surrounding the Homestead. Frank Baldwin, a skilled craftsman in a Watertown, Connecticut brass foundry, made the teapot circa 1910 for Frank Wood, owner of the Homestead. The design was based on a teapot that had been in the Wood family for years.

At the foot of the green are three mounted Revolutionary War cannons acquired by American arms merchants in France. These were among forty-five pieces a Swiss captain brought to Edenton in 1778 since the British blockade made delivery to the intended ports too dangerous. Twenty-two made their way up the Chowan River to Virginia.

Chowan County Courthouse
117 East King Street
1767
National Historic Landmark

Standing at the head of the Courthouse Green since 1767, the Chowan County Courthouse is one of the most important surviving buildings from the colonial period in North Carolina. The oldest courthouse still in active use in North Carolina, it has always been used for many purposes. Here Edenton citizens met during the struggle for independence. It was the county's seat of government for over two hundred years, and the venue for many public meetings, religious services, and a wide range of social activities.

Based on classical British architecture and built by local artisans using local materials, the T-plan building is laid in Flemish bond brick over an English bond water table. The entrance leads directly into the courtroom. The assembly room that is sometimes called the ballroom occupies the central portion of the second story.

Several notable figures and events from Edenton's history are associated with the building. Joseph Hewes was one of the commissioners appointed to raise money for its construction. James Iredell and Samuel Johnson pleaded their cases before judges presiding here. When President James Monroe visited Edenton in April 1819, citizens gathered here to honor him with a dinner.

Although no documentation supports the theory, circumstantial and stylistic evidence suggests English architect John Hawks, who designed Tyrone Palace in New Bern, may have designed this building. Most official functions were moved to the new building on South Broad Street in 1979.

The North Carolina Courthouse in Raleigh and the Chowan County Courthouse are the only places where the North Carolina Supreme Court can convene.

Jailer's Residence (former)
1905

Chowan County Jail (former)
1825

115 East King Street

The Jailer's Residence is a modestly finished brick Victorian dwelling that was erected by the county as the home of the keeper of the Chowan County Jail at a cost of $2,050. Conveniently located between the jail and the Courthouse, the jailer occupied the building until the early 1970s.

The Chowan County Jail is the oldest documented jail in North Carolina. Built in 1825, it was the fifth jail in the county, with earlier prisons erected around 1722, 1741, 1788, and 1809.

The brick structure, raised in English bond, has front and rear walls which are 29 inch thick on the first story and 24 inches thick on the second story; the end walls of each story are 18 inches thick. Steel cells, added in 1905, remain essentially unaltered. This jail was used until the new regional jail was built in 1979–1980.

James Iredell House
105 East Church Street
Circa 1773
National Register of Historic Places

In December 1756, John Wilkins acquired the four lots at this site, which he sold to silversmith Joseph Whedbee in 1773. Whedbee built the two-story gale-front section on the east before selling it to James Iredell, Sr. in 1778.

Covered with beaded weatherboards, the one-bay building had a single exterior chimney. The interior side-hall plan house may have been an expansion of Wilkins' circa 1756 house, thus explaining the gable's atypical orientation to the street.

Deputy Collector for the North Carolina Port of Roanoke at 17, Iredell was Attorney General of North Carolina at 28. When he was 38, George Washington appointed him as an Associate Justice of the United States Supreme Court. In 1773, Iredell married Hannah Johnston (1748-1826), sister of future Governor Samuel Johnston, Iredell's law tutor.

During the early nineteenth century, Iredell's widow added the two-story center-hall plan block on the west. The house remained in Mrs. Iredell's possession until her death in 1826, and in her daughter's estate until 1870.

Saved in 1948 by the Edenton Tea Party Chapter, National Society Daughters of the American Revolution, the house is owned and managed by the State of North Carolina. The James Iredell Association assisted in restoring and furnishing the building.

The circa 1829 Bandon Plantation office, now furnished as a school, was moved in 1964 in appreciation of novelist Inglis Fletcher, who wrote part of the Carolina series here. Although the Bandon Plantation house was destroyed by fire in 1964, the kitchen was deconstructed and moved here in 2009. Reconstruction was completed in 2013.

St. Paul's Episcopal Church
100 West Church Street
Circa 1736–1774
National Register of Historic Places

Organized under the provisions of the Vestry Act of 1701, St. Paul's was the first parish in the colony. The original building, erected in 1702 east of Queen Anne's Creek, was a post-in-ground structure. By 1736, when the old church had outgrown its usefulness, the parish commenced building a new church in Edenton, then the bustling capital of the colony. The resulting structure, North Carolina's second oldest church building still in regular use, is a landmark in the development of religious architecture in the state.

Though the parish was in sympathy with the cause of the American Colonies, the Revolution had a disastrous effect on St. Paul's as the Anglican denomination fell into disfavor and funds from England ended. By the 1790s, the building had fallen into bad condition although it was used occasionally. In 1805, a group of local churchmen began to raise funds for repairs. They hired William Nichols, an English architect from New Bern, to plan the restoration; he was responsible for the addition of the spire.

The interiors remained relatively unchanged until 1848, when the present chancel woodwork and furniture were designed by another English architect, Frank Wills of New York. One of the leaders in the Gothic Revival movement in the United States, he so respected the Romanesque forms of the apse and the barrel-vaulted ceiling that he used the same motifs in his design.

In 1949, during further repairs, the steeple, roof, galleries, and old organ were destroyed by fire. As all interior furnishings and memorials had been removed and stored before repairs started, they were installed again when the church was rebuilt exactly as it had been before the fire.

St. Paul's Episcopal Churchyard
100 West Church Street
1722–present

When Edenton was incorporated in 1722, two acres were set aside near the center of the town as the church lot and churchyard. Since the Anglican Church was established by law in the colony, it was the church's responsibility to provide burial for the citizens of the town. Burials in the churchyard were taking place for more than a decade prior to the construction of the church here in 1736.

Because there was no natural stone in the area, the earliest burials remained unmarked or were marked by either brick vaults or wooden markers which deteriorated through the years. While the lack of gravestones creates an unoccupied appearance, the churchyard is quite full of graves, whether presently marked or not.

St. Paul's remained Edenton's only cemetery until the early nineteenth century, when the newly organized Methodist (1808) and Baptist (1817) congregations established graveyards adjacent to their buildings. Even so, the churchyard at St. Paul's was being filled at such a rapid rate that in 1829 the vestry passed several "Regulations respecting Interments in St. Paul's Church-Yard, Edenton." The regulations provoked a storm of criticism, for the churchyard had always been the town cemetery, with free and unrestricted burials.

By 1851 the vestry was appealing to the town council to provide another cemetery. This did not occur until 1889, when the formation of Beaver Hill Cemetery on West Albemarle Street relieved the demand for burial space at St. Paul's. Burial in the old churchyard was eventually limited to the descendants of families already interred there, and is, at present, restricted to local members who have their family buried here.

Interned are members of many families prominent in local history including three colonial governors under the Lords Proprietors, Henderson Walker, Charles Eden for whom Edenton was named, and Thomas Pollock.

The surviving gravestones at St. Paul's reflect funerary art and traditions that span 240 years. The oldest marker, the slate stone of Margaret Davison (1733–1753), displays rare early North Carolina example of the winged cherub that was common in New England gravestones of the seventeenth and early eighteenth centuries. Few monuments are as eloquent in expressing unfulfilled potential as the stately obelisk marking the grave of Augustus Moore (1803–1851), on which a finely articulated cedar tree is snapped in half.

The few gravestones In St. Paul's churchyard that are signed by the stonecutters are from the large cities with which Edenton carried on the majority of its commerce, primarily from Norfolk, Baltimore, and Philadelphia.

Enclosed by a handsome brick pier and paling fence, the churchyard at St. Paul's is one of the finest in the state. Its important collection of funerary art is rivaled in eastern North Carolina only by Calvary churchyard in Tarboro. Its lush planting of trees and shrubs give it the appearance of a small botanical garden.

Located at the churchyard's western boundary is the Rector's study, a small one-room building erected around the 1850s.

Josephine N. Leary Building
421-423-425 South Broad Street
1894

The impressive triple-story building was erected in 1894 as a rental property for Josephine Napoleon Leary, born into slavery in Williamston, North Carolina in 1856. Mrs. Leary and her husband, Sweety Leary, came to Edenton by the mid-1870s. Both were barbers by trade, and Mrs. Leary was listed in various business directories from 1883 until 1912. Mr. Leary was only listed in directories in 1890.

Pressed metal façade buildings were popular throughout North Carolina during the late nineteenth and early twentieth centuries. The metal façade was manufactured by the Mesker Brothers, Front Makers, located in St. Louis, Missouri. The building has eight bays and is composed of three sections. Each unaltered storefront has recessed double-leaf doors. Victorian embellishments adorn the outside of the building along with columns framing the second story, massive bracketed frieze and cornice, and elaborate sunbursts. The interior spaces remain largely unaltered. The name Leary and date 1894 adorn the top of the façade. A Victorian color scheme enhances the design of the façade.

The Learys lived at what is now 102 South Broad Street. This two-story structure was razed in the 1960s. Mrs. Leary also owned other properties including the Williams-Flury-Burton House (ca. 1779) located at 108 North Granville Street. Mrs. Leary, a remarkable businesswoman, died in 1923; Mr. Leary died in 1905.

Cupola House
408 South Broad Street
1758–1759
National Historic Landmark

Francis Corbin arrived in Edenton in 1750 as the land agent for the first of the English Lords Proprietors, Robert Carteret the Earl of Granville. In the seventeenth century, Carteret acquired vast territories south of Virginia from King Charles II. Earl Granville instructed Corbin to have a safe office in Edenton for the storing of documents and transacting business. Corbin acquired the Cupola House lot in 1756 and built the house in 1758.

The house is considered to be the finest wooden-type Jacobean house south of Connecticut and North Carolina's most significant early dwelling. The cupola was designed for both ventilation and observation of the harbor.

Dr. Samuel Dickinson purchased the house from the Corbin heirs in 1777. A native of Connecticut, Dr. Dickinson moved to Edenton by 1767 where he established a large medical practice. Mrs. Elizabeth P. Ormond, who later married Dr. Dickinson, was one of fifty-one women who signed what has come to be known as the Edenton Tea Party resolution on October 25, 1774.

Descendants of Dr. Dickinson called the Cupola House home for 141 years. With very meager financial resources in 1918, the last of the Dickinson line, Miss Tillie Bond, sold the elaborate Georgian woodwork on the first floor to a representative of the Brooklyn Museum of Art, where it remains today.

Alarmed about losing part of the town's history, the citizens of Edenton established the Cupola House Association (CHA) to purchase and protect the property. This was the earliest community preservation effort in North Carolina to save a historic structure. For the next forty-five years the county library occupied the Cupola House. Both a tearoom on the first floor and a museum on the second floor operated to raise funds to support the property. The house is a two-and-a-half story architecturally significant building featuring an octagonal cupola, which is covered in rusticated siding (wood cut to imitate stonework). Two large chimneys anchor each side of the house. The structure features wooden weatherboards and heavy shingles on its gabled roof.

Ornate mantels and woodwork can be seen throughout the interior of the building. The balustrade of the staircase in the central hallways features carved floral decorations and moldings. The doors leading to the two main rooms extend up to the ceiling. The furnishings are period pieces with a few of Dr. Dickinson's belongings, one the 1780 tall case clock found in the central hallway. Reproduction of the lost woodwork occurred in 1965 with the cooperation from the Brooklyn Museum of Art. The 1960s also saw the opening of the building as a museum.

The Cupola House was designated a Registered National Historic Landmark in 1971. It is owned and operated by the Cupola House Association. Tickets may be purchased for guided tours of the home at the Edenton Visitor Center Tuesday through Saturday.

Gardens of the Cupola House
408 South Broad Street
1758 to present

Gardens are once again an important part of the Cupola House. Francis Corbin, who built the house in 1758, and the Dickinson and Bond families who occupied the home for 141 years had planted gardens. Unfortunately, by the time the Cupola House Association (CHA) organized to save the house most of the gardens were lost.

After purchasing the property surrounding the Cupola House in 1973, the CHA began turning the space into gardens. Using a 1769 map drawn by C. J. Sauthier as a guide, Gertrude Shepard Rosevear generously donated funds, gardening knowledge, and endless time to establish the gardens. Improvements included the orchard beside Water Street, the elegant arbor, and an herb garden and vegetable plots in the back of the house. In the spring and fall of 1976, professionals and garden club members installed the gardens. Following seventeenth century kitchen garden practices, the herb garden's design reflects the pattern of the lower panels of the house's doors.

To counter the usual challenges of establishing and maintaining gardens, a group of volunteers began working in the gardens on Wednesday mornings. This group, affectionately named the "Weeders," continues to care for the gardens.

The Cupola House Weeders received one of the governor's special Volunteer awards in 1996. Frances Inglis has received two honors for all of her work and efforts in the gardens. The first award was in September 2013, when the Cupola House Board of Directors unanimously voted to name the gardens in honor of Frances Drane Inglis. A plaque in her honor was placed on the arbor. Mrs. Inglis was again honored for all of her work in re-creating the gardens by the Southern Garden History Society who presented its certificate of merit to her on February 28, 2014, at their annual meeting held in Savannah, Georgia. The award reads, "For contributions to the appreciation, understanding and preservation of Southern Garden History."

The gardens are open to the public daily. Tickets may be purchased for guided tours of the home at the Historic Edenton State Historic Site. To learn more about the Cupola House, the gardens, or the association please visit www.cupolahouse.org. The website has a database of the flowers, shrubs, herbs, and trees planted in the garden.

Roanoke River Lighthouse
Water Street and Edenton Bay
1903

The Roanoke River Lighthouse may be the last remaining square screw-pile lighthouse. At one time, there were fifteen screw-pile light stations along North Carolina's inland waterways. This lighthouse greeted travelers and ships navigating the waters of the Albemarle Sound into the Roanoke River. No records exist indicating what happened to the original lens.

Decommissioned and abandoned by the U.S. Coast Guard in 1941, the lighthouse remained vacant for approximately 15 years. Elijah Tate purchased it and then sold it to boat captain and underwater salvager Emmett Wiggins. He transported the lighthouse to Edenton and placed it on land at the mouth of Filbert's Creek. Wiggins lived in the lighthouse until 1995, and it remained in his family after his death.

Using a grant provided by the North Carolina General Assembly, the Edenton Historical Commission (EHC) purchased the property on May 15, 2007. The North Carolina Department of Transportation used federal stimulus funds for the exterior restoration. On May 1, 2012, the lighthouse was moved to its permanent location over the water. EHC raised the funds to furnish the interior.

Beaded tongue-and-grove boards cover the interior walls. The first floor consists of an entry hall with a staircase to the second floor, parlor, kitchen, and office. Two bedrooms take up the second floor space. The interior is furnished with period pieces appropriate for a lighthouse and its keeper. The outhouse can be found of the east side of the structure's balcony.

The Historic Edenton State Historic Site located at 505 South Broad Street provides public tours of the lighthouse. For additional information please visit www.edentonlighthouse.org.

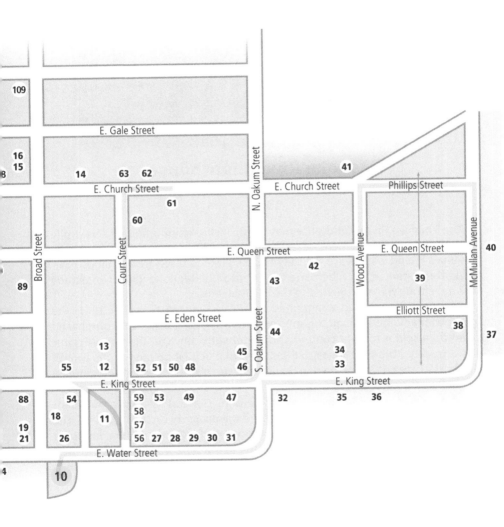

E. Gale Street

109

16
15
8

14   63   62

E. Church Street

N. Oakum Street

E. Church Street

41

Phillips Street

61

60

Court Street

E. Queen Street

Broad Street

89

42

43

E. Queen Street

39

40

Wood Avenue

McMullan Avenue

E. Eden Street

Elliott Street

44

38

37

13

45

34

33

55   12

52 51 50 48

46

S. Oakum Street

88   54

59 53   49   47

32   35   36

18

11

58

57

56 27 28 29 30 31

19
21

26

E. King Street

E. King Street

E. Water Street

4

10

24

East Side and Mill Village Trail

10	Barker House
26	Homestead
27	William J. Leary House
28	McDowell-Holmes House
29	Millen-Hathaway-Francis House
30	Brown-Elliott House
31	Charles A. Wood House
32	Orthodox Church (former Suffolk and Carolina Railroad Depot)
33	Edward Piland House
34	William Seay Cabinet Shop
35	John Tyler Page House
36	Superintendent's House
37	Edenton Cotton Mill
38	Edenton Cotton Mill Office
39	Mill Village
40	First Christian Church
41	Edenton Peanut Company
42	Oldest House in North Carolina
43	Edenton Public School (former)
44	John R. Wheeler House
45	Jane C. Page House
46	Owens Bunch House
47	Barrow Hole House
48	James Coffield House
49	Privott-Jones House
50	Haywood C. Privott House
51	Howard B. Chappell House
52	Bateman-Badham House
53	Hatch-Bruer-Davis House
54	Frank Wood Building
55	Leary Law Office
56	Julien Wood House
57	James A. Woodard Jr. House
58	Skinner-Bond House
59	East Customs House
60	Edenton Graded School, Edenton High School
61	St. John the Evangelist Episcopal Church (former)
62	Skinner-Elliott House
63	Edenton Academy (former)

Homestead
101 East Water Street
1771

Constructed on land used for commercial purposes as early as 1718, the house was built in 1771 by Robert Smith who was a merchant partner of Joseph Hewes. Smith and Hewes were friends of the colorful sea captain John Paul Jones, and many believe Jones may have stayed in the house. Josiah Collins of Somerset Plantation purchased the property in 1786, and mainly Collins descendents have occupied the house since then.

The Homestead, as it has been known since at least 1842, is the only surviving Edenton house with double porches on all four sides in the West Indies manner. The distinctive scalloped front porch fascia is original. The front and back doors are aligned so that breezes from the bay can blow through the house and, when open, allow a view from Water Street to East King Street. One-story wings on each side are 20th century additions and replace a Victorian era addition that at one time stood on the east side.

The large property is filled with distinctive plants including a huge magnolia tree in the front garden which is nearly two hundred years old and an exquisite perennial and herb border that extends over two hundred feet from the rear entrance to East King Street. Three outbuildings that were originally a smokehouse, kitchen and barn remain in the back garden and date to the mid-nineteenth century.

Near the fence facing the Courthouse Green a commemorative tea pot sits on top of a Revolutionary War era cannon. This marks the site of a house that was once imagined to have been the site of the 1774 Edenton Tea Party.

William J. Leary House
203 East Water Street
1897

This house and the one at 304 South Granville Street exemplify the Queen Anne style in Edenton. The home was based on a design by George F. Barber of Knoxville, Tennessee, closely related to "Design No. 1" of Barber's pattern book *The Cottage Souvenir No. 2 – A Repository of Artistic Cottage Architecture and Miscellaneous Designs* (1891). The owners, being quite pleased with the appearance of the home at 304 South Granville Street, wanted their new home to reflect the same finishing elements.

The house was built on the site of the family's prior home. The new home includes parts from the old home: an old staircase, seven doors, two marble mantels with three grates and slate hearths, and exterior siding used on the rear of the house. Newer elements include wood-shingled gables, extensive porches, and a three-stage octagonal tower. Stick Style accents appear on the tower and the frieze above the second story windows. Crowning the entire composition are ornamental finials and crockets at the ridge of the hip roof, the tops of the gables, and the pinnacle of the tower.

The interior follows an asymmetrical plan, focusing on the entrance hall and an intricate screen above the arched entrance to the rear hall. The arch is echoed by a wider and more modest version in the upstairs hallway. Mantels throughout the house are ornate.

McDowell–Holmes House
205 East Water Street
Circa 1820

While little is known about the early history of this Colonial Revival style home, architectural elements inside the house include raised six-panel Georgian doors and wide three-part Federal surrounds. The broad end-gable roof, one surviving pilaster with molded capital, and some beaded weatherboarding indicate early elements. The original house, therefore, likely dates to the 1820s.

Renovations in the 1880s added a one-story wing and a Victorian porch. A photograph from 1890 documents the Victorian influences. Renovations in the 1920s created the Colonial Revival appearance of today. The house gained a front pedimented gable and side boxed cornices, a two-story bay window on the west, and the deep porch carried by Tuscan columns. The east bay window was moved to the second floor over the entrance. Additional renovations updated the home's interiors.

Millen-Hathaway-Francis House
207 East Water Street
Circa 1775

In 1722, Patrick Ogilby secured from the Commissioners a lot on which his daughter's family would live until 1744. Scottish merchants, Question Millen and Hugh Morris bought it in 1722, and Millen built the older part of the present house around 1755. A Loyalist, Millen had to leave the country during the Revolution, entrusting his family to the care of friends who were political foes.

Originally a two-story single-pile frame house, the three-bay façade, double-tier porch, brick exterior end chimney, gabled roof, and side-hall plan were typical of 1775. Even though the house was renovated at least three times, various original elements remain, including several nine-over-six and six-over-six sash windows and the double shouldered Flemish chimney.

Evidence points to a late nineteenth century addition of an east elevation two-story recessed wing, which was expanded in the early 1900s. The wing was expanded again in the early 1900s to add the projecting front gable.

James Robert Bent Hathaway, "an exceptionally well read person" likely occupied the home for his entire life. His strong interest in North Carolina history led him to establish the quarterly *The North Carolina Historical and Genealogical Register,* more commonly known today as *Hathaway's Register.* The set of eleven issues is an important source of genealogical research for North Carolina.

Brown-Elliott House
209 East Water Street
Circa 1905

Frank Fred Muth, a German native new to the area in 1905, constructed this attractive Colonial Revival home, for Miles Gilbert Brown (1875–1927), a successful industrialist. Mr. Brown's saw and planning mill was then located directly to the east of the home. Successful completion of this home led Muth the builder and Brown the lumberman to collaborate on the construction of several others dwellings. Brown maintained this house as a rental, never living there himself.

The design features a prominent front pediment enclosing a semi-circular window. The shed-roof porch rests on Tuscan columns with paneled pedestals. Windows near the spacious entrance foyer display Muth's most noted trade-mark, the use of colored glass in both the trabeated entrance and at the stair landing. The colorful motif is of stylized irises. The corner blocks reflect the Art Nouveau period.

Charles H. Wood House
211 East Water Street
1918

A formal example of the Colonial Revival style, this large, double-pile home built by Frank Fred Muth features a prominent hip roof, a pair of dormers, modillion brackets, and paired windows. The house's original stylish porch sheltered only the entrance and consisted of paired Doric columns supporting an entablature articulated with triglyphs.

The house, originally built on 109 South Broad Street, was moved to its current location after being condemned in 1977, to make room for construction of the new courthouse.

After its move, the new owners added the Colonial Revival style wraparound porch and a two-story rear addition.

The town was established in 1712 on the north shore of the Albemarle Sound as "The Towne on Queen Anne's Creek." It was renamed Edenton a decade later in honor of Governor Charles Eden.

Orthodox Church
(former Suffolk and Carolina Railroad Depot)
300 East King Street
Circa 1902

This building with its prominent hip roof is thought to be the passenger depot built around 1902 by the Suffolk and Carolina Railroad. It was moved to this location between 1910 and 1920. Other than its roof, nothing of the original character survives.

While the structure's original location is not certain, it may have stood in the 300 block of East Church Street, which is where the Norfolk and Southern Railroad built a passenger depot in 1910. The Norfolk and Southern Railroad gained control of the Suffolk and Carolina Railroad in 1906. The 1910 passenger depot survived until about 1970. In recent years, the structure has been used as a church.

---

*The train tracks on East King Street are remnants of
the Suffolk and Albemarle (1902), the second
railroad to arrive in Edenton.*

Edward Piland House
307 East King Street
Circa 1785

The house is a late eighteenth century example of the gambrel roof style. Originally located northwest of Gatesville, North Carolina, it was built for Edward and Susannah Piland on their 300-acre plantation located on a main road leading from Buckland to Wynns Ferry on the Chowan River.

Peter Piland inherited the house and surrounding 300 acres, subject to his mother's dower interest. The property passed through several hands until 1851 when James and Nancy Lawrence along with their two minor children, Martha Ann Lawrence and Mills Kindred Lawrence, purchased the house. Martha, who married Job Hofler, inherited the house. Their daughter, Mary, married Thomas Lassiter in 1878, and their names have been associated with the house in modern times.

The house was empty for several decades before the current owners purchased it in 2010. The house retains its original wainscot on both floors, as well as its original interior and exterior window and door architraves. The first floor contains eleven-foot ceilings, an unusual feature for a house of this style and period. The house's interior was originally painted Prussian blue, and a fragment of early, if not first period, wallpaper was located in the enclosed staircase. A second floor bedroom retains early wrought nails that originally secured a floor cloth.

In the 1970s, the house's four original raised panel mantels and raised panel overmantels were sold out of the house. Detailed measured drawings were created from photos, allowing them to be recreated by Edenton master cabinetmaker, Don Jordan. Land was not available for the house to be restored on site, so its owners chose to relocate it to Edenton, where it serves as a reminder of a house style once common to the town.

William Seay Cabinet Shop
Rear of 307 East King Street
Circa 1790

The small building that now sits behind the Edward Piland house is the only known, purpose-built 18th century cabinet shop in the American southeast. Built in 1790 by William Seay, the cabinet shop was discovered in a field just east of Roxobel, North Carolina. Research indicates the field was part of Seay's plantation; Seay began his career as a house joiner in the 1770s.

After his father's death in 1774, William Seay expanded his house joining enterprise, constructing homes for wealthy plantation owners within a 25–mile radius of Roxobel along both sides of the Roanoke River including Hope Plantation in Windsor. The furniture making aspect of his business greatly expanded in 1790 when he received a large commission for the construction of corner cupboards, presses, and at least one desk from wealthy planter Whitmell Hill. Hill instructed Seay to place his initials,"WH," on the surface of these pieces, which were intended as gifts for his children and for Hill's personal use. This commission necessitated the construction of the cabinet shop. From this point until his death around 1812, Seay took a personal interest in the construction of some of the most extravagant furniture ever made in North Carolina.

The cabinet shop probably continued to be used for its original purpose for at least some period after Seay's death. By the 1830s, however, it was converted into a house. The building continued to be used as a small house until the 1920s, when a single story addition was added to its front. By 2011, the cabinet shop had fallen into extreme disrepair. Its restoration and placement in Edenton greatly enhances the prospect for its survival in the future.

John Tyler Page House
308 East King Street
Circa 1883

John Tyler Page (1852–1901) and his wife, Hessie (Collins) Page, were both born into slavery as members of the Collins family. Although Page was a carpenter, little is known about his building career. Their daughter, Harriet (Page) Gorham (1882–1966) inherited the house and after moving to New York would return to spend summers in her family home.

This first mention of a house on this property occurred in 1782 when mariner Thomas Cox purchased four lots which included several buildings. From 1794, the home changed hands several times until 1883 when John Tyler Page (1852–1901) bought it. Mr. Page dismantled the old house and erected a Victorian one. He built this interesting home on the original Flemish bond brick foundation and used the chimney, mantel, and doors from an earlier house on the site. A surviving mantel suggests the original house was constructed during the last quarter of the eighteenth century. Local tradition holds the home's Georgian elements were salvaged from area homes being demolished or updated.

During the early 1990's a renovation was started. The parties involved had a falling out and the property was sold. Prior to the sale most of the interior had been stripped down to the bare studs. Two of the original mantels, one door and the flooring remained. Descriptions of these missing design elements appear in Thomas Butchko's book, *Edenton: An Architectural Portrait*. The present owners were unable to retrieve any of the original 1883 materials. Today this home has been refurbished with contemporary interiors while exposing what features remained in their original condition.

Superintendent's House
400 East King Street
1909

Homes for workers and supervisors were built alongside the Italianate-Revival style cotton mill. The one-and-a-half-story home for the superintendent is built in the Colonial-Revival style. Architectural features include gambrel and pedimented rooflines, two bay windows, and a spacious front porch. The garage on the left side of the house was built in 2014. The property backs up to the Queen Anne Creek.

Other nearby Cotton Mill related houses are the Engineer's House built in 1908 at 310 East King Street, the Supervisor's House built in 1921 at 312 East King Street, the Spinning Overseer's House built in 1914 at 401 East King Street, and the Carder's House built in 1916 and at 403 East King Street.

The Edenton Cotton Mill has 700 feet of hallway and lobbies.

Edenton Cotton Mill
715 - 723 McMullan Avenue
1899

Nineteen local residents, who saw a great future in providing a market for the region's cotton growers, formed the Edenton Cotton Mill in August 1898. The project's architectural firm, C.R. Makepeace and Company of Providence, Rhode Island, was one of the foremost designers of textile mill buildings. Edenton Brick Works provided the machinery to make the bricks on site.

The mill's design, derived from the Italianate-Revival, is an example of the large brick industrial complex once popular in North Carolina. The building's defining feature is the 180 large segmental arched windows and projecting ceiling joists, which create light inside the 100,000 square foot interior.

Ownership of the mill remained in local hands until 1993 when Pioneer Yarn Mills of Sanford, NC. Unifi of Greensboro acquired the mill. The closing of the mill in 1995 caused the loss about approximately 70 jobs and created an uncertain future for the industrial building.

Town Councilman Samuel B. Dixon, a board member of Preservation North Carolina (PNC), asked PNC to help connect Edenton with potential buyers. While attending the PNC's 60th anniversary, physician and real estate developer Dr. Thomas Wilson learned of the opportunity to purchase the mill. Events moved quickly, and PNC persuaded Unifi to make a donation of the 44 acres and building. Dr. Wilson purchased the mill and began development.

The Raleigh, North Carolina architectural firm Clearscapes won the Gertrude S. Carraway Award of Merit for their work converting the Edenton Cotton Mill into 30 high-end condominiums. While each of the units varies in size and layout, the exterior of the building is maintained in accordance with historic-district guidelines.

Edenton Cotton Mill Office
420 East Elliott Street
1909

Edenton is home to one of the most well preserved intact mill villages in the State of North Carolina. The entire village is listed on the National Register of Historic Places.

The Edenton Cotton Mill Historic District consists of 57 mill houses (1899–1923), a brick office building, an impressive industrial building (1899), and the First Christian Church (1916).

While the cotton mill was built in 1899, the office was not constructed until 1909. The board of directors authorized funds for the building of the modest Victorian brickwork structure. The Colonial Revival porch was added later. The office building is a handsome complement to the large mill structure; particularly interesting are the office's segmental arched windows which echo the much larger windows of the mill. The two-room interior housed one room for secretaries and sales and the other for executive offices.

The office doubled in size in the 1950s with the Colonial Revival addition on the west.

In 2014 and 2015, restoration of the outside of the building included the fence surrounding the property and landscaping.

The building currently houses the Cotton Mill Museum. A 2005 homecoming of "Cotton Mill Kids" conceived the idea of preserving the history of the Mill and the people who lived and worked there. The museum was established in 2008. The museum is open every Saturday and Sunday from 10 am to 2 pm. For further information please visit the museum's website at millvillagemuseum. org. The property is privately owned.

Mill Village

McMullan Avenue, East King, Elliott, East Queen, and Phillips Streets
1899–1923

The Mill Village homes were built for the employees or "operatives" as the mill management referred to their workers. The minutes from the mill state that the first "tenements" were to be built in May 1899. The homes found on the south side of Queen Street and the north side of Elliott Street are the oldest of the mill houses.

Although the village contains both one- and two-story vernacular wood-frame homes, the majority of the homes are simple one-story three-room structures. Many of the structures were built as duplexes with each side consisting of one room and a shared kitchen. The mill assigned workers to the dwellings primarily based on family size and the number mill employees in the family.

Since the majority of the mill workers were former farmers, a large expanse on each block behind the homes allowed the mill workers to cultivate gardens. Today the area still displays lush areas of trees and grass behind the homes.

The Greensboro-based company Unifi donated the mill and the mill village to Preservation North Carolina (PNC) in 1995, which then sold the homes. *Cottage Living* Magazine named The Edenton Cotton Mill Village as one of the Top 10 Cottage Communities in 2007. Today all of the homes in the village are single-family dwellings with several retaining their original two-front-door design.

The land at the corner of McMullan and King Streets, set aside for a baseball diamond for recreational purposes for the mill workers, is a large park available for town events.

First Christian Church
703A McMullan Avenue
1916

Although built in 1916, religious services for the mill workers began in 1906 when the company set aside this lot for a church and contributed $100 to the Methodist Episcopal Church South to assist in the building's construction. Beginning in 1909, quarterly payments of $100 were approved to cover the expenses of what was called "Factory Mill Church." In 1915, the sum of $100 was donated towards the building of a Sunday school room.

Modest elements of the Romanesque Revival church include the corner bell tower and the round-arched windows on the first floor inset with colored glass. The exterior was brick veneered in the 1960s. A small frame building, seen behind the church, was erected in 1949 as a Sunday school annex and now houses social rooms and a kitchen.

The building is still in use today as a church.

---

*The inside of Edenton Cotton Mill has
100,000 plus square feet.*

Edenton Peanut Company
East Church Street
1909
National Register of Historic Places

Established on January 19, 1909, the Edenton Peanut Company was at the forefront of the peanut industry in North Carolina. By the 1930's it was the largest peanut market in the state and the second largest in the world. The company had approximately 100 employees, the majority of them black women with the exception of the managers, foremen, and office staff.

Mr. James Wood of Edenton served as president of the company during World War II. The company's flagship product "Jimbo's Jumbos" was named for Mr. Wood. The company shipped five-pound bags of peanuts to every Chowan County service member Mr. Wood could locate. Edenton Peanut Company received thank you letters written to Mr. Wood, other company officers, and the company. There is a collection of 29 letters from men and women stationed across the United States dating from June and July 1943 that describe service life, geography, and social interactions during the beginning years of the war.

The five-story building is the tallest in town. Architecturally, the style of the structure reflects the popularity of the American industrial buildings derived from northern Italian prototypes. Originally, the first story of the building was used for peanut storage, the second story for picking, and the third and fourth for polishing, and the fifth for hoppers. The building remained vacant for almost 50 years. Rehabilitation of the building was made possible when a father and son team purchased the property in 2006. The repurposed building is now home to thriving businesses and a fitness center.

Oldest House in North Carolina
304 East Queen Street
1718–1719

In 2010, new owners purchased this house intending to make it a rental cottage. At the time locals believed the house dated to the 1910s. While removing old 1960s interior paneling, workers discovered evidence of an older house. Bead board paneling indicated the house was built during the late 1800s.

After noticing the wood below the area where an old chair rail had been removed, the contractor revealed yet another house layer. At this point all restoration stopped, and Preservation North Carolina came in to access the structure and advise the owners about the building's preservation.

Several scientists, historians, and other experts have studied the house. Excited by the find and armed with knowledge about the building techniques that emerged, they formed many theories about its history. A dendrochronologist's evaluation of wood samples from the structure indicates the house dates to the winter of 1718 and 1719.

Archeological digs indicate the house has been in its present location for the last two hundred years. Some speculate the house was originally located closer to Queen Anne's Creek and later moved north as the commercial activity increased along the waterfront. Evidence also shows the interior stairs were moved five different times.

Long term plans will revolve around showcasing the house's educational potential. It will remain in private hands until a suitable permanent protection can be developed.

Edenton Public School *(former)*
205 South Oakum Street
Circa 1851

This small Greek Revival building was the first public school for whites built in Edenton. Its construction began in 1851, but was delayed a few years due to lack of funds. The school committee urged the doubling of the school tax, challenging the county court by saying, "We shall discharge our duty – discharge yours…" The building was completed in 1856.

The three-bay structure is covered by a low hip roof defined by plain pilasters that rise to carry an equally plain entablature. The nine-over-six windows are original, but the porch and trabeated entrance were later modifications. The side wing and rear ell were added after school trustees sold the building in 1904.

Church bells and the courthouse bells were melted during the Civil War to make the cannons for Edenton Bell Battery.

John R. Wheeler House
301 South Oakum
Circa 1901

This home with ornate front trim possesses one of the most imaginative uses of Victorian millwork in the state. The double-tier porch is supported by turned posts. The detailed woodwork resembles a lacy veil and includes turned spindles, balusters, pendants, sawn brackets and scrolls, and drilled moldings.

The spindle-work friezes support bands of wave-like scrolls. The astronomical motif in each of the panels flanking the porch posts incorporates sawn representations of the sun, moon, a planet, and a comet. While lore holds that Haley's Comet inspired the comet shape, it appears the panels were created before Haley's Comet was visible in 1910. The front and side gables also contain elaborate sawn decorations.

The rear of the home contains two separate kitchens, one for summer and another for winter. Originally the kitchens were connected to the house by a large porch; the summer kitchen remains detached.

The first English exploration of the area in 1586 from the Roanoke settlement found two Algonquian tribes, the Chowanoke and the Weapemeoc, along the Chowan River.

Jane C. Page House
306 South Oakum
Circa 1881

This modestly scaled, undecorated Gothic Revival home is the finest example of such homes in Edenton. The house illustrates the combination of a vernacular form with subtle Gothic Revival elements, which can be seen in the steep pointed wall dormers on the front façade. The plain features are common to similar homes in the Edenton area.

Most homes of this genre were built for aspiring members of Edenton's black community. This one was built after May 1881, when the lot was purchased by Jane C. Page, the widow of John R. Page, a prominent citizen in the black community and leading carpenter from the post Civil War period. It stayed in the family until 1948, when it was willed to St. John the Evangelist Episcopal Church, which owned it until 1959.

---

*The Badham family was a group of African American
architects, builders, and carpenters who
called Edenton home.*

Owens Bunch House
308 South Oakum Street
Circa 1909

Furniture store owner Willis Owens (1879–1918) bought this corner lot in January 1909 and built this Colonial Revival style home within the next year. The corner lot shows off this L-plan house which features a wrap-around porch carried by Tuscan columns from the entrance to the end of the rear ell. A second story porch augments the ell. The entrance moldings indicate the builder as Frank Fred Muth, an established Edenton builder.

The interior is handsomely finished, with fine mantels and open stringer stair. An exceptional built-in china cabinet in the original dining room occupies the place of a mantelpiece and echoes the form and character of the south parlor overmantel.

The original owner died during the influenza epidemic. The house changed hands a few times but was restored and occupied again in 2014.

———————

*The Chowan County Courthouse was first platted in 1712
and stands as the oldest continuously used courthouse
in the United States.*

Barrow Hole House
216 East King Street
Mid 1700s

This house, which may have been built as early as 1743, was originally erected in the rural Center Hill area of northern Chowan County. The name Barrow Hole Swamp goes back to around 1700, well before the earliest grant of land on which this house originally stood. The large single room with a loft home may have been moved more than once.

In 1983, the house was moved to its current location and renovated to reflect a mid eighteenth century appearance. As it is one of only a few eighteenth century one-room homes in Edenton, it offers an idea of a type of home and style of finish that were probably common of the period.

As was common with these very small homes, this one included a story-and-loft with an asymmetrical three-bay composition and six-over-six sash windows with heavy one-inch-wide muntins. The single room was likely portioned into the hall and parlor plan during the later half of the 1800s.

The Supreme Court of North Carolina can only hold sessions in either the State Capitol of Raleigh Courthouse or the Chowan County Courthouse.

James Coffield House
209 East King Street
Circa 1764

The James Coffield House is one of the most imposing homes in Edenton. While the home's present appearance dates largely from expansion during the 1830s, the 1974 restoration revealed an older house at the core as well as the original foundation of marl, or coquina, a stone-like composition of shells, the use of which was very rare in the Albemarle region.

Today the house is a large two-and-a-half-story, double-pile center-hall plan. The beaded floor joists on the porch and modillion cornice at the eaves date from the 1830s, and the elegant chamfered posts and delicate balustrade are 1974 replacements for Victorian elements.

The house may have been the home of Margaret Lavinia Coffield and her husband Dr. Thomas D. Warren during the construction of their new home, Wessington (120 West King Street). The home, then known as Bond's Inn, was used as a boarding house during World War II, when housing was greatly needed due to the influx of Marines at the training base.

Privott-Jones House
208 East King Street
Circa 1892

The starter home of Haywood C. Privott, who would later build the large brick house across the street at 205 East King, this dwelling contains numerous Queen Anne details including tall windows, high downstairs ceilings, intricate porch details and an asymmetrical design accented by a diminutive upstairs porch. The sidelights and transom around the front door are enhanced by stained glass added in the 1980s.

Though the original front section of the house remains one of Edenton's least altered examples of a modest Queen Anne style, a rear addition designed by Charleston architect Martin Meeks was added in 1987. The addition repeats the detailing of the front and includes a porch that replicates the posts, railings and moldings of the front porch.

---

*Edenton was home to James Iredell, an Associate Justice
of the first United States Supreme Court.*

Haywood C. Privott House
205 East King Street
1900

A noteworthy example of the Queen Anne style, this home was built for Haywood Cullen Privott (1862–1931) and his wife, Georgia Leora (Byrum) Privott (1869–1943). Banker, businessman, and Clerk of Court, Mr. Privott was also a director of the Edenton Cotton Mill. In 1900, he purchased 20,000 bricks left over from the construction of the mill and used those to build his home.

The dwelling is very similar to the 1897 built William J. Leary House at 203 East Water Street, suggesting Privott may have borrowed the plans George F. Barber drew for the Learys. The same contractor likely built both houses.

Because of the home's brick medium, its presence relies primarily on the strong, asymmetrical design rather than decorative embellishments. The corner tower provides a focal point with its dentiulated cornice, slate shingles, flared skirt, and robust metal finial. The deep porch originally terminated with an octagonal pavilion that served to balance the tower.

The home's interior is massive in scale, with tall ceilings, heavy moldings, and robust mantels of Neo-Classical Revival style. Dominating the entrance is a Tudor arch enclosing a ball-and-spindle screen. The handsome stair is augmented by a distinctive built-in bench.

50

Howard B. Chappell House
203 East King Street
Circa 1911

This pleasant house, an example of the Colonial Revival style, is similar in style to at least two others in town. Shortly after buying the lot in 1911, Howard B. Chappell (1880–1956) had the house built. The house's original form was very similar to one at 100 West Gale Street and the Spinning Overseer's House at the Cotton Mill.

The 1919 modification added the second story sleeping porch on the front west. At the time, sleeping in the open air was considered a primary recuperative treatment for tuberculosis, which the owner's son was suspected of having. Mr. Chappell resided there until his death, and the house remained in the family until 1980.

Joseph Hewes was a signer of the Declaration of Independence and called Edenton home.

Bateman-Badham House
201 East King Street
Circa 1879

This house is one of the few surviving Edenton houses from the period between the Civil War and the arrival of the railroad in 1881. The house originally included a decorative two-tier porch with bracketed cornices and robust window pediments, which gave the house a stylish Victorian appearance. The window pediments are very similar to ones on the Norfleet-Privott House at 117 West Church Street.

The 1920 remodel rebuilt the porch with fluted Doric pillars in the Colonial Revival style. After 1972, the second-story balustrade was removed and interior woodwork was added.

The Chowan County Courthouse built in 1767 has been characterized as "The finest example of Georgian architecture in the South."

Hatch-Bruer-Davis House
200 East King Street
Circa 1744

The lot where this house stands was part of the property which Governor Charles Eden sold in 1722. The home began life as a one-and-a-half story side-hall plan structure in 1744, on a lot purchased in 1741 by a French barber, André Richard. The original section of the house consists of the western three bays.

At one time thought to be the oldest dwelling in Edenton, the home was later enlarged resulting in a two-story center-hall structure. The renovations could have happened in the 1780s or between 1800 and 1804.

Evidence of these early changes may be visible on the west exterior chimney where the lower portion was erected with small bricks laid in an English bond. As part of the two-story addition, the English bond was supplemented with Flemish bond. Later changes included common bond, a twentieth century replacement.

The Chowan County Courthouse built in 1767 is the oldest continuously used courthouse in the nation and is recognized as a National Historic Landmark.

Frank Wood Building
114-116 East King Street
Circa 1890s

This brick rental building began as a one-story structure built on a corner of the residential lot by Frank and Rebecca (Collins) Wood, the owners of the Homestead (101 East Water Street). These offices were built specifically for attorney William Dossey Pruden Sr. His sons and grandson practiced law there until 1956.

The second-story, added between 1904 and 1910, was headquarters for the Chowanoke Club, a men's social club organized in 1906 by thirty of Edenton's leading white citizens. They met here until they disbanded in the early 1930s. The building continues to be owned and maintained by descendants of the original owners.

When North Carolina ratified the United States' Constitution in 1789, 13 lanterns were hung in the cupola of the courthouse. Twelve were lit leaving one unlit for Rhode Island who had not yet ratified the constitution.

Leary Law Office
105 East King Street
Circa 1882

This small Victorian building was erected for William J. Leary on land purchased by his wife, Emma Woodward Leary. He and his sons practiced law here for many years, and the family owned the building for almost a century.

Small buildings like this one were common in Edenton until the twentieth century, although only two remain today (the other is the Skinner law office at 401 Court Street, enlarged to become a residence). These small buildings were usually the offices of professional men or the shops of craftsmen. They were often located next to the family home, allowing one to work from home while remaining separate from the bustle of home activities.

Generally these tiny buildings contained two rooms, with a door to the street and a step or two at the threshold or a small porch. This specimen is brick with a stucco gable front with corbels in the raking frieze and a wooden cornice carried by brackets.

The town served as North Carolina's colonial capital from 1722 to 1743 and, with a natural port, prospered as a hub of commerce, political, and social activity.

Julien Wood House
409 Court Street
Circa 1890

This richly ornamented Victorian house was erected between 1885 and 1893 for Julien Wood (1863–1943), the son of Edward Wood Sr. of Hayes Plantation. Mr. Wood soon married Elizabeth Benbury Badham (1870–1938) and served many years as the first president of the Bank of Edenton.

The house displays robust millwork, including bracketed cornices, bracketed window hoods, and extensive use of sawn moldings exhibiting fleur-de-lis and egg-and-dart motifs. The house was originally built with separate porches on three sides, but by 1904 the street elevations were unified by the present Colonial-Revival wrap-around porch.

The interior features a handsome Victorian stair and a variety of Victorian and Colonial-Revival woodwork.

---

*Double porches are prominent in many
two-story frame homes in Edenton.*

The James A. Woodard Jr. House
407 Court Street
1910s

A fine example of the one-and-a-half story Bungalow, this house was erected in the 1910s for James A. Woodard Jr. (1866–1938), a merchant and grocer, and his wife, Annie (Bond) Woodard (1871–1944). Characteristic Bungalow elements include the broad gable roof highlighted by a distinctive shed porch, now enclosed, on the second story, the use of wood shingles, and the deep engaged porch.

The distinctive entrance surround, along with the interior stair, indicate that the house was built by Frank Fred Muth. The informal interior plan is finished in a stylish Colonial-Revival manner. The living room features a Neo-Georgian mantel with a raised overmantel.

In 1774, fifty-one women lead by Penelope Barker boldly signed their names to a document protesting the British king's taxation. Unlike the members of the Boston Tea Party who dressed in disguise, the Edenton women did not hide their identities.

Skinner-Bond House
405 Court Street
Circa 1790

The first known owner of the lot was Governor Charles Eden, who sold it in 1722. Six years later it was bought by James Trotter, a tailor, who in May 1743 gave half to his "beloved friend," Mrs. Martha Hoskins Potter, a widow. The two were married in December of 1743. Trotter descendants owned the property until after the Revolution.

The original part of the present house was acquired in 1803 by Joseph Blount Skinner who greatly enlarged it shortly after his marriage a year later. The earliest part of the house had a double-tier porch that was probably expanded by architect William Nichols circa 1810. One of the leading citizens of Edenton during the first half of the nineteenth century, Skinner was a lawyer and progressive farmer who followed modern scientific agricultural practices.

In 1846 it was sold to Henry A. Bond, who modernized it from Federal to Greek-Revival style. Bond's descendants and relatives owned it until 1973.

East Customs House
401 Court Street
Circa 1790

On property first owned by Governor Charles Eden and later by James Trotter, tavern keeper, Mrs. Mary Wallace (Trotter's daughter), lived until 1792. All of her property was sold before 1803, but her house was standing on this corner until the spring of 1807. It was soon replaced by Joseph B. Skinner's (1781–1851) law office, probably designed by William Nichols. The core of the current Colonial-Revival structure is Skinner's two-room law office.

After Henry Bond bought the property in 1846, it was used for some time as the Customs House, doctor's office and private school for girls during the late nineteenth century. About 1920, it was greatly enlarged to its present size by Bond's granddaughter, Mrs. Clara Preston. It is believed that the work was done by Frank Fred Muth who was very adept at remodeling older structures into the Colonial-Revival style. The Prestons, the first people ever to reside in the old office, lived here until their deaths.

Edenton Graded School, Edenton High School
100 Block Court Street
1916

The majestic Colonial Revival style building with its Flemish bond brick provided modern school facilities for Edenton's white children. The flanking wings
were added in 1926, and a large auditorium was added to the rear in 1930. First
known as the Edenton Graded School and then Edenton High School, it remained the local high school until construction of the present John A. Holmes
High School in the 1950s.

Repurposed as an elementary school and named in honor of Ernest A.
Swain, a longtime educator and principal, the building remained a school until
1985 when the elementary school was consolidated with the D. F. Walker Elementary School.

In 1988, the front portion of the school was deeded to Winston-Salem developer DeWayne Anderson, who created 38 apartments. This project was a
joint endeavor of the developer, Chowan County, and the Historic Preservation
Foundation of North Carolina, Inc. The building has been recognized as one
of the more successful and exemplary adaptive reuses of school buildings in
the state of North Carolina. Chowan County retains ownership of the auditorium, which was renovated, and today is used for a variety of civic activities.
The basement houses the Chowan Senior Center.

St. John the Evangelist Episcopal Church (former)

212 East Church Street

1881

This Gothic Revival structure exemplifies the partnership of church and school in Edenton's black community during the late nineteenth century. The parish was organized April 6, 1881, as a mission church, on the same day of the church building's consecration. St. Paul's Episcopal Church lent support and encouragement to the new congregation, and Herbert Henry Page, owner of the house now known as Pembroke Hall, donated money for the building.

In 1884, a tornado almost demolished the building, leaving just enough of the framework to serve as the skeleton for the present building. This new building was consecrated on May 22, 1887.

The interior is among the finest in a nineteenth century black church in eastern North Carolina. Spanned by trusses, the sanctuary focuses on the exquisite chancel and rood screen.

To the east of the church is the former St. John School, begun in 1892; the present building dates from 1902. This school is the only survivor of the three black sectarian schools that operated in Edenton during the late nineteenth and early twentieth centuries.

Because of a dwindling congregation, the church was deconsecrated by the diocese and is now rented to another congregation.

Skinner-Elliott House
201 East Church Street
Circa 1830

Records indicate that a dwelling was erected on this site for carpenter Richard Whedbee soon after his purchase of the lot in December 1774. What became of this earlier house is not known, and there is no visible indication that an older house is contained within the present one.

In 1826, James C. Johnston of Hayes gave the property to George Blair's daughter Elizabeth (1802–1852) when she married Joshua Skinner Jr. (1797–1852). This present house was probably built for them within several years and the Skinners occupied it until 1836.

The large two-and-a-half-story side-passage plan house is representative of the comfortable dwellings erected in Edenton during the first third of the nineteenth century. With its double-tier front porch engaged beneath the sweep of the gable roof, the dwelling displays uncluttered lines, original nine-over-nine windows, and a pair of interior brick chimneys.

---

*James Iredell of Edenton was the youngest member of the
first United States Supreme Court at the age of 38.*

Edenton Academy (*former*)

109-111 East Church Street
1800; separated 1895

This pair of identical gable-front dwellings once comprised the former Edenton Academy, which opened in 1801 on the nearby Court Street site now occupied by the E. A. Swain Apartments. When a large new Victorian building was erected in 1895, the old Academy was cut in half and moved to this lot, where each section was remodeled as a separate dwelling. The facades of the two present dwellings butted each other in the center of the original building.

The Edenton Academy had received a charter as early as 1770, but little is known about the original building. The school was reorganized in 1800 with Samuel Johnston as president. By 1810, girls were also being admitted and within twenty years the female enrollment was larger than the male.

Building before being separated

W. Albemarle Street

112   111   110   109

W. Gale Street   E.

114   113
117 116 115   101 103 104 105 106 108   16
15
14

W. Church Street   E. C

118   100   102   107
119
120   99 98 97 96 94 91

W. Queen Street

122   95 93 92 90
121   89

Moseley Street   Broad Street

80 79 78 77

W. Eden Street

81   76
82   75   74 71 70 68 66   55   13
12

Blount Street   Granville Street   W. King Street   E.

83   73 72   69 67 88   54   11
18
19   26
85 21

W. Water Street   E. V

84   10

23

Edenton Bay

64

Teapot Trail

James Iredell Jr. Law Office
Edmund Hoskins Store
104 West King Street
Circa 1802

This house was built for merchant Edmund Hoskins. It is an important example of a building that was enlarged twice within a short time of its original construction and illustrates the transition between Georgian and Federal woodwork in Edenton. The earliest section is the front room of the gable-front block on the East side. It was formerly used as Edmund Hoskins Store and is the oldest building once used commercial purposes. Hoskins continued to run his store here after he had sold the property to James Iredell Jr. in 1816. In 1820 Iredell took it over for his law office.

James Iredell Jr. (1788–1853) was one of Edenton's leading figures during the 1810s and 1820s. His father James Iredell Sr. (1751–1799) was well known as a political leader during the Revolution and as a justice on the first United States Supreme Court. The son, who represented Edenton in the North Carolina General Assembly in 1813 and again from 1816 to 1828, was Speaker of the House 1817 to 1827. In 1828 he was elected Governor and moved to Raleigh. He resigned that position to finish out the term of Nathaniel Macon in the U. S. Senate. He sold the house in 1829 to the State Bank of North Carolina.

The house had a series of owners since. The present owners have done extensive work to restore and expand this lovely home.

Joseph Hewes House
105 West King Street
1756

Previously known as the Disbrowe-Warren House, this handsome residence is Edenton's prime illustration of an early house that has been modified, stylistically dated, and enlarged by a succession of owners in its two and a half centuries of existence.

In 1775, George Disbrowe bought two lots from Susanna Cockburne of Edinburgh, Scotland. Although there were outbuildings on the property at the time, Disbrowe had a house built the following year, little of which remains visible today.

Disbrowe's house was purchased in 1778 by the business firm of Hewes, Smith, and Allen as an investment property, and it remained entangled in estates until 1794. One of the owners, Joseph Hewes (1730–1779), was one of Edenton's foremost Revolutionary patriots, a signer of the Declaration of Independence, and promoter of the Navy.

The house as it appears today dates primarily from two later periods. Frederick Norcom, who owned the house from 1810 until 1838, updated the front to reflect the Federal style. Dr. William C. Warren, who owned the house from 1838–1863, added the rear ell in 1851 and updated the interior with Greek-Revival elements.

Wagner-Wood House
106 West King Street
1851

The deeds for this property give more details about domestic property than any others recorded in Edenton. In 1742, when Joseph Blount was living here (he did not own it), the outbuildings included a store house, a "fowl house," and a stable. By 1760, the property changed hands, and the 1769 Sauthier map shows a house located close to the street. In 1816 James Iredell Jr. bought the property and the one east of it.

The house as it stands now was built for David D. Wagner in 1851. Whether he ever occupied the house is uncertain. After 1856, it belonged to Edward Wood and his descendants until 1994. During this time the house was moved back on the property. Several owners have since renovated and restored this beautiful home.

The present house, an austere example of the Greek-Revival style, was built as a single-pile dwelling. The house was enlarged to double-pile by the adding a tier of rooms across the rear. The porch, the house's distinguishing element, is supported by handsome Doric pillars raised on wooden pedestals and enclosed by a Victorian balustrade. The interior of the house features a spacious center hall that terminates at the rear with a handsome stair rising from an oversized newel.

Elliott-Sitterson House and Dairy
107 West King Street
1895

Mr. William O. Elliott built this house as a two story rental property in 1895. The home was occupied by the family of Mr. E. S. Norman. The focus of this house is the handsome Victorian double-tier porch embellished with turned and sawn balusters, spindle work frieze, brackets, pendant drops, and fascia moldings. Completing the exterior are scalloped and drilled moldings on the window hoods and intricate gable ornaments. A two-story ell and simply finished double-tier porch expand the rear.

The house was sold in 1901 to James C. Sitterson and his wife Corinne (Broughton) Sitterson. In 1949 Mrs. Sitterson sold it to her neighbor Joseph H. Conger who maintained the property as a rental until 1984. The house has since been thoroughly renovated. It is maintained today as a privately owned residence.

The Dairy located behind the house is of considerable significance. Built during the late eighteenth century, it displays one of only three known examples of brick nogging to survive in Edenton. Nogging, the infill of wall cavities in frame structures with brick as a means of insulation, was a traditional European practice that found infrequent application in coastal North Carolina. In this case, it served to keep milk products as cool as possible.

Bennett-Dixon House
110 West King Street
Circa 1780s

This large, modestly finished two-and-a-half-story side hall plan dwelling was erected for William Bennett, soon after he purchased the lot in 1780. The next owner, a cabinetmaker, added a double tier of rooms at the rear and advertised it as a workshop. The house originally had a double-tier porch and stood within ten feet of the street.

The home's owners in 1927 removed the double porch and added the ell, side porch and sun porch. In 1933 the house was sold to John Augustus Moore (1878–1947) and his wife. Moore came to Edenton in 1931 as general manager of the Edenton Cotton Mill. The couple resided in the house until their deaths.

Their daughter Elizabeth Vann Moore resided in the home until her death in 2010. Elizabeth's love of Edenton and her passion for its history is responsible for much of the research and writings for this guide book. The home has been recently been beautifully restored by new owners.

Frank Fred Muth was instrumental in building or renovating many Edenton homes.

Beverly Hall
114 West King Street
1810

The original structure was a two-story single-pile hall-and-parlor plan with a large ell on the rear northwest. It was built for John Bonner Blount and his wife Margaret (Mutter) Blount as their residence and his private bank. In 1816, the State Bank of North Carolina purchased it for a branch bank. In 1855, however, William Badham purchased the building and began modifications to create the house as it stands today.

Although a Union major briefly occupied the house during the Civil War, the Badhams resided here until their deaths, and Dr. Richard Dillard, Sr. bought the house in 1876. Dr. Dillard renamed the house Beverly Hall in honor of his wife, Mary Louise Beverly (Cross) Dillard.

The Dillards were succeeded by their son Dr. Richard Dillard, Jr., who was succeeded by his nephew, Richard Dillard Dixon, Clerk of Court for many years.

In 1941, Dixon was appointed to serve as a special Supreme Court Judge for North Carolina. In 1946, he went to Nuremburg, Germany to assist in the war crime trials. He presided at four trials before coming home in 1948 to resume his career in law. The house remains in family ownership.

The interiors of Beverly hall have been restored to create a comfortable family home with a great respect for its history. Inside the house, the original bank vault both surprises and delights visitors.

The gardens are very special. The present owner is an avid gardener and historian. He has recreated beautiful garden rooms and paths. His interest in preservation has led to several outbuildings being brought to the property and restored. Beverly Hall and the surrounding gardens are often opened to the public for various community events.

Skinner Paxton House
115 West King Street
Circa 1820s

In 1798 merchant Samuel Butler built a building on the lot and advertised it as a new rental property for thirty five pounds per year. The present house is either the original house, which was dramatically remodeled, or a new building.

The largest and most stylishly finished side-hall plan house in Edenton, the two-and-a-half story house is anchored by a pair of interior end chimneys on the west. The double-tier rear porch, original in form, is carried by monumental Doric pillars which are enclosed by a balustrade of slender balusters. The front porch was added in 1960–1961 in the Federal Revival style. The interior boasts exceptional woodwork throughout.

In recent years, new owners have added on a family wing overlooking the sound, installed a new kitchen, and restored and updated the main living areas of the house, including adding work and family space to the basement. The exterior grounds have been beautifully landscaped and maintained. The rear entrance to the property on Water Street is particularly lovely. During the springtime, blooming cherry trees line the driveway.

Pembroke Hall
121 West King Street
1850
National Register of Historic Places

Standing on a bluff overlooking Edenton Bay, Pembroke Hall is a fine example of the Greek-Revival style in North Carolina. The simplicity and clarity of the exterior, with its double-tier porticoes on front and rear, are enriched by use of academic Greek-Revival detail. Many of the elements, including the columns of the second level of the portico and those in the hall, are based on plates from *The Beauties of Modern Architecture* by Minard Lefever.

The house was built for Dr. Matthew Page (1801-1853) and his second wife, Henrietta Elizabeth (Collins) Page (1811-1868). Their son, Herbert Henry Page, erected the building for St. John the Evangelist Episcopal Church.

Gertude Murray (Shepherd) Rosevear purchased the house in 1947 and renamed it Pembroke Hall. She was a driving force in the restoration of the Cupola House Gardens.

The interior's gracious scale and handsome proportions continue with Greek-Revival styling. The focus is the broad central hall that extends between the front and rear porches. The family and service areas are finished in a less elaborate Greek-Revival manner.

The grounds retain vestiges of what must have been fine Victorian gardens. Dominating the front lawn is a venerable American beech with limbs that rest on the ground.

In 2010, a group of citizens formed Pembroke Hall Preservation Partners LLC to acquire and save the house. Since 2011, a special use permit allows limited rental of the house and grounds for receptions and events to help defray maintenance costs.

Wessington
120 West King Street
1850–1851
National Register of Historic Places

Wessington is a landmark example of eclectic design in antebellum North Carolina. The grandest house in Edenton was built for Dr. Thomas Davis Warren (1817-1878) from plans adapted from William H. Ranlett's *The Architect*, Volume I, published in 1847. The kitchen wing was added in 1866. The lacy iron balconies make a fine contrast to the sturdiness of the house.

The porch is approached by a stair flanked by cast iron railings and pair of ornate lanterns. The double-pile center-hall plan interior is extraordinary in its size and finish. The hall is approximately fifty feet long, twelve feet wide and fourteen feet high. The stairway's location in a side hall leaves the hall open from front to back.

Dr. Thomas Warren arrived in Edenton in the mid-1830s. During the Civil War, he served as a surgeon with the North Carolina troops. The Warrens fled Edenton in 1862, and Federal officers occupied Wessington during his absence. Dr. Warren suffered great financial losses during the war and returned to Edenton to practice medicine. By 1869, he sold the home to John C. Williams of New York, who allowed the Warrens to share the house with him until Dr. Warren's death.

Later owners of the home were descendents of George Washington and named the home Wessington after the first president's ancestral home in England. Members of this family occupied the home until 2008.

Within the last few years Wessington has undergone extensive renovation. The new owners have brought Wessington into the twenty-first century while retaining all of its nineteenth century character.

Dixon-Powell House
304 South Granville Street
Circa 1895

One of the finest Queen Anne style residences in the Albemarle region, this impressive house epitomizes the scale and sophisticated detailing that made the style a favorite of ambitious homeowners during the nineteenth century. The design is a masterful blend of the asymmetrical massing, juxtaposed gables, porches, dormers, corner pavilions, and textural wall finishes that were hallmarks of the Queen Anne style. The most outstanding feature is the circular pavilion at the southeast corner of the porch, covered with a patterned slate roof and crowned by a metal finial.

The interior illustrates late Victorian interior design in its full glory. The height of the rooms is accentuated by over-sized doors. There are numerous examples of exquisitely crafted mantels. A handsomely carved staircase is carried by stylish turned balusters.

Erected for successful merchant Minton Hughes Dixon (1849–1923) and his wife, Sallie (Dillard) Dixon (1859–1910), the house was built by Theo Ralph, probably based on a plan by George F. Barber of Knoxville, Tennessee, one of the country's most prolific architects of the period. While Mr. and Mrs. William J. Leary were building a similar home at 203 East Water Street, Mrs. Leary specified several times that her new home should have finishing elements like Mrs. Dixon's.

Dixon-Williams House
300 South Granville Street
Circa 1925

This handsome Colonial Revival style house was built for Richard Dillard Dixon and his wife, Louise Manning (Badham) Dixon. The design focuses on a handsomely detailed coved pediment that shelters the central entrance. The modillion cornice is repeated on both the house and the dormers, where arched windows echo the entrance roof.

Dixon, the Clerk of Court for many years, grew up in the adjacent home of his father, M.H. Dixon. He and his family did not occupy their new home long, however, for in 1928 he inherited Beverly Hall from his uncle, Dr. Richard Dillard Jr., for whom he was named.

The Gothic Revival style appears chiefly in churches.
St. Anne's Church, however, contains some
surprisingly Romanesque elements.

Charlton–Warren House
206 West Eden Street
1761–1769

This home was built for Jasper and Abigail (Slaughter) Charlton. He, a successful lawyer, was active in Revolutionary politics; she was the first signer of the Tea Party resolutions.

The house has an asymmetrical three-bay façade with a shed porch framed into the structure of the building. Entrance onto the porch is by stairs at either end. A double paved shoulder chimney raised in Flemish bond anchors each end. Of special interest are the brick "ears" found behind each shoulder. The rear elevation contains shed rooms which were enlarged between 1904 and 1910. A one-room wing was probably added within twenty years of the house's completion. The back wing is a recent addition.

Eugene I. Warren, a later owner, was a man who loved to tinker. He rigged a string from the chicken house door to the wall above his bed so he could let the chickens out in the morning without getting out of bed.

───────◆───────

*Edenton was the first permanent settlement in what is
now the state of North Carolina.*

Borritz-Tredwell-Muth House
214 West Eden Street
Circa 1787

The house was built for Swiss sea captain William Borritz soon after he acquired the lots in 1787. From 1799 to 1826 the house was home to Samuel Tredwell (1763–1826), the customs collector of the port of Roanoke, and his wife Helen (Blair) Tredwell (1763–1802). During the mid-1800s the house was owned by William C. Wood. In 1911 it was purchased by Frank Fred Muth (1860–1936), Edenton's leading contractor from 1905 until his death and his wife Maria (Falter) Muth (1863–1954).

This house has had many renovations. The 1988 renovation revealed the nature of changes that had occurred. While many of the original floorboards remain, most of the interior and exterior woodwork, including the porch and mantels, is new or substantially reworked. The original chimneys remain, and the original porch was probably replaced early in the nineteenth century. The overall effect of the changes made over the years creates a very handsome home.

———————

The grand opening of the first railroad was held on
December 13, 1881. In the next eleven months,
it carried 11,000 passengers.

Byrum–Jackson House
216 West Eden Street
1896

The double-tier porch on this Victorian house exemplifies the decorative possibilities of one of Edenton's most important late nineteenth century architectural features. It provides a lace-like veil to the traditional two-story single-pile, frame dwelling. Especially noteworthy are the distinctive star motif brackets that accent the turned porch posts and anchor a complex sawn and drilled frieze molding. The sawn and drilled molding repeats in the frieze of the roof, where it serves to crown the entire design.

The house was erected in 1896 for farmer and fishery owner Octavius Coke Byrum and his wife Sarah Ida (Basnight) Byrum. They bought the property in January and sold it eight months later to Sarah R. Stacy. The next month, the Byrums acquired the lot a 109 West Queen Street where they built a similar house.

Large parts of Edenton were declared a
National Historic District in 1973.

Littlejohn-Byrum House
218 West Eden Street
1790

Exhibiting the classic Edenton double-tier semi-engaged porch, this large single-pile dwelling exemplifies local domestic architecture during the late eighteenth century. It was built around 1790 for William Littlejohn (1740–1817), then Commissioner of the North Carolina Port of Roanoke, and his wife Sarah (Blount) Littlejohn (1747–1807), one of the of the Tea Party resolutions.

Anchoring the house is a pair of impressive double-paved shoulder chimneys raised in Flemish bond. Handsome three-part molding encloses the raised-six-panel door and transom. The center-hall plan interior with high ceilings is among the finest Federal interiors in Edenton.

The house passed through several hands before being purchased by hardware merchant Thomas Campbell Byrum (1892–1968). He and his wife, Lillian D. (Forehand) Byrum (1894–1968) Byrum resided here until 1949. Their son, Thomas Campbell Byrum Jr. (1922–1987) then purchased the house. It remains in family ownership.

G. W. Spry House
219 West Eden Street
Circa 1922

Erected for G. W. Spry (1875–1926) soon after his purchase of this lot in September 1922, this building is an especially pleasant example of the modest gable-front bungalow. Distinctive elements include the tripartite gable window, composed of a central vertical four-over-one sash window flanked by narrow louvered vents, an element seen on several homes in north Edenton, and the front porch where the railing, instead of being supported by balusters, rests on a low weatherboard wall.

Spry died shortly after the house's completion, and his widow, Mary V. (Banks) Spry (1877–1949) remained there until her death, as did their son, Roy L. Spry (1900–1954). The home has undergone major restoration and renovation in recent years; it remains a private residence.

Edenton is a small unique town known for its authentic eighteenth, nineteenth, and early twentieth century public buildings and homes.

West Customs House
108 Blount Street
Circa 1772

This two-and-a-half story house is a handsome example of the comfortable dwellings erected for successful Edentonians at the dawn of the struggle for independence. Anchored on the west by a pair of brick chimneys raised in Flemish bond with paved double shoulders, the house is covered with beaded weatherboards. The raised six-panel door greets visitors, and the multiple paned windows adorn the outside.

Local lore holds that merchant Wilson Blount had the house built shortly after he purchased the lot in 1772. He sold the home in 1777, and customs collector Samuel Tredwell (1763-1826) bought it in 1799. For the next seventy years the Blount Street house was known as the Customs House.

The double-pile side-hall floor plan interior is remarkably spacious given the home's seemingly modest size. The staircase, in the center of the hall, is simply finished and rises to the attic. Interior finishes boast molded chair rails with simple beaded baseboards. Mantels in the home are handsomely executed with a molded shelf and shaped frieze in the front parlor and delicately scaled reeding and broad molded shelves on the upstairs mantels.

The property has one original remaining outbuilding, the smokehouse that dates from at least the early nineteenth century. The traditional double-tier front porch with Greek-Revival Doric columns was added in the 1830s or 1840s.

More modern renovations include the 1930s addition of a one-story porch and bedroom on the east side of the home and a small kitchen off the northwest side of the home. Additionally, the house was moved to its present location on the lot in 2003 to make room for the garage that has two bays with a room and bath above.

Ice House
101 Blount Street
Circa 1840

The Ice House built in the 1840's, was located on commercial waterfront property owned by Henry Alexander Bond. Later it was inherited by his son, Millard Filmore Bond. The building was used as an ice house until the 1900s. Several owners later, it was sold to H.C. Privott in September 1919. The Privotts ran a farm equipment/mercantile business in the 1920s. Mrs. Anne Graham, the owner of Wessington, purchased the property in the early 1930s. The building stood vacant until 1980, when it was converted into a studio apartment.

The General Assembly of North Carolina in 1961 created the Edenton Historical Commission. Edenton and Chowan County have continued to play a role in the preservation and perpetuation of history in the colony and State of North Carolina.

C. E. Kramer Garage
113 West Water Street
Circa 1920

Eugene Irving Warren built the garage so that it could be rented to Carroll Edward Kramer (1887–1950) for his general automobile repair business. Warren sold the building to Kramer in 1923. The structure is the last remaining early automobile garage and service station in Edenton.

The building also housed the first consolidated Edenton Fire Station. The fire company occupied the front of the structure while the garage occupied a rear portion of the building, which no longer stands. One chief and sixteen men, partly paid and on duty during the daytime, made up the first volunteer fire department.

Architecture of the building is one of a simple design with a prominent parapet decorated with tiers of corbelled brick. The outside of the building also has simple brick pilasters and stuccoed lintels that provide interest to the brick walls.

Edenton Bottling Company
112 West Water Street
Circa 1908

This structure was built for Edenton Bottling Company proprietor Reubin Madrin. The elongated one-story brick building with a rear second story features a tall, stepped parapet façade and a simple scheme of decorative brickwork. The later is limited to corbel lintels and simple recessed panels flanking a central louver in the upper façade. A native of Elizabeth City, Madrin began his Edenton career in 1901 while working for a bottler from his home town. He soon began a business on his own and at first carried a general line of soft drinks. Mr. Madrin added the Chero-Cola line in 1922 and Nehi products in 1925. He sold his products throughout the immediate Albemarle region and as far away as Currituck County.

His heirs sold the property in 1954. Since then it has served the community as many different businesses including, but not limited to, an antique shop, real estate office, and restaurants. There is an apartment in the second story section looking over the Albemarle Sound. Today the first floor serves as a retail property.

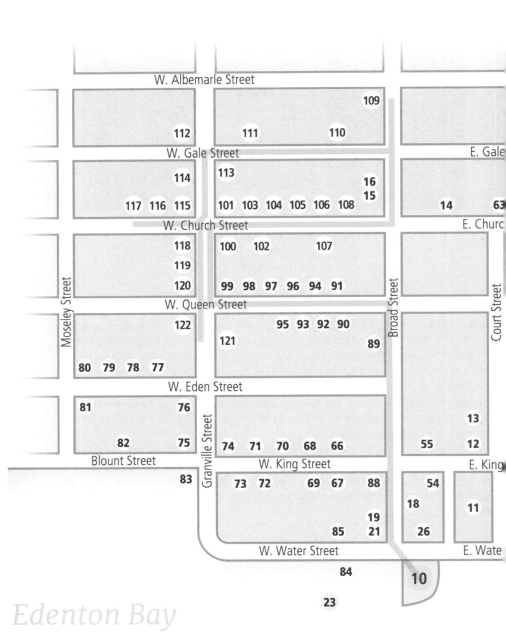

W. Albemarle Street

109

112   111   110

W. Gale Street   E. Gale

114   113
                                              16
                                              15
117 116 115   101 103 104 105 106 108   14   63

W. Church Street   E. Churc

118   100   102   107

119

120   99 98 97 96 94 91

W. Queen Street

122   95 93 92 90

121   89

80 79 78 77

W. Eden Street

81   76   13

82   75   74 71 70 68 66   55   12

Blount Street   W. King Street   E. King

83   73 72   69 67 88   54
                                   18
                        19   11
                85   21   26

W. Water Street   E. Wate

84

10

23

Edenton Bay

86

Heart of Edenton Trail

10	Barker House
88	Town Hall (former Bank of Edenton)
89	Taylor Theater
90	Mitchell-Wozelka House
91	Miller-Sutton House
92	O. C. Byrum House
93	Murden-Brown House
94	Bond-Lipsitz-Small House
95	Rea-Vail House
96	Skinner-Chappell House
97	Pruden-Goodwin House
98	Leigh-Hathaway House
99	Leigh-Bush House
100	William Scott Privott House
101	William D. Pruden Sr. House
102	Leila Major White House
103	Folk-Taylor House
104	Edmund R. Conger House
105	C. S. Vann House
106	Robert B. Drane House
107	William M. Bond House
108	St. Paul's Episcopal Church Rectory
109	St. Anne's Roman Catholic Church
110	Samuel F. Williams House
111	Gale Street Baptist Church
112	Walter S. White House
113	Booth House
114	James N. Pruden Sr. House
115	Bond-McMullan-Elliott House
116	Rea-Miller House
117	Baker-White House
118	Paine House
119	Twine-Satterfield House
120	Dr. Henry M. S. Cason House
121	Goodwin-Leggett House
122	Edenton Baptist Church

Town Hall
400 South Broad Street
1911

A fine example of the Neo-Classical Revival style, the Town Hall was first built as the Bank of Edenton. The two-story brick and stone structure conveyed the sense of fiscal responsibility represented by the first bank organized in Edenton after the Civil War and was considered to be one of the most handsome and best equipped banking homes in eastern North Carolina.

The land for the building was purchased from Miss Tillie P. Bond in 1910, and the architect was Charles Collins Benton of Wilson, North Carolina. Constructed out of reinforced concrete and faced with limestone veneer, the magnificent exterior belies the building's modest interior.

In June 1986, the bank donated the building to the Town of Edenton. The town of Edenton renovated the first floor offices for the town's mayor and municipal staff.

Taylor Theater
206-208-210 South Broad Street
1925

The Colonial Revival and Neo-Classical Revival styles of the Taylor Theater make it one of the finest small theaters remaining in eastern North Carolina. The one-story façade is divided into sections with the central entrance flanked by two shops.

Inside, the proscenium arch retains remnants of the Colonial Revival in this building designed by Charles Collis Benton, a leading architect in eastern North Carolina. Originally opened as an opera house, it was converted into a twin cinema around 1980, but closed in 1987, only to reopen in 1990.

Technology threatened to shut down the screens permanently, as the needed new digital equipment cost $150,000. Citizens of Edenton rallied around the owners of the theater to help raise the necessary funds. A town-wide kickoff party was held in November 2012 to "Save the Taylor." Citizens and businesses wrote checks totaling $50,462 and the mason jars that were set up around town netted another $7,185. Two local businessmen presented the mayor of Edenton a donation check for $100,000, completing the funds required to save the theater.

The effort on behalf of the citizens and businesses of Edenton is just one of many examples of how much effort is put into keeping Edenton a viable and special place to live. The Taylor Theater continues to be part of the fabric of the town.

Mitchell-Wozelka House
105 West Queen Street
Circa 1877

Built in the plan of a Greek cross, this house is the most outstanding domestic example of the Gothic Revival in the Albemarle region. The interior consists primarily of two main rooms in the center of the house with the lateral arms of the cross serving as twin entrance halls.

It was built for Robert G. Mitchell who came to Edenton in the late 1850s and married Sarah Cheshire, the daughter of an Edenton merchant. The house remained in the Mitchell family until 1890, when it was sold to John M. Wozelka and his wife Mary.

Natives of Vienna, the Wozelkas came to Edenton in the 1870s and operated a bakery at the southwest corner of Broad and Queen Streets.

The house has been divided into three apartments.

The Taylor Theater is one of the finest small theaters in North Carolina still standing.

Miller-Sutton House
108 West Queen Street
Circa 1919

This impressively scaled residence is one of the best examples of the Bungalow style in Edenton. The uncommonly wide overhanging eaves of the roof, dormers, and porch create a distinctive profile. Resting on Doric columns and tall entablature, the roof's dramatic sweep covers the deep wrap-around porch.

The interior has a spacious entrance hall separated from the parlor by a handsome screen of raised pillars and pilasters. False ceiling beams in the dining room continue the Bungalow elements.

Edenton resident, Joseph Hewes, was appointed the first
Secretary of the Navy in 1776. John Adams said that Hewes
"laid the foundation, the cornerstone of the American Navy."
Hewes also signed the Declaration of Independence.

O. C. Byrum House
109 West Queen Street
Circa 1896

The Victorian house, following traditional forms with double tier porches and distinctive decorative features, was built for Octavius Coke Byrum (1874–1919) and his wife Sarah Ida (Basnight) Byrum (1874–1960). The Byrums had built a similar house at 216 West Eden Street.

The house and porch follow traditional forms. The turned porch posts are embellished with bull's eye medallions, while sawn work accents the roof frieze, porch fascia and bracketed window hoods. The interior focuses on a pair of nearly identical Victorian mantels.

Mr. Byrum died in the influenza epidemic in 1919. His widow continued to reside here until her death forty-one years later.

---

*The earliest inhabitants of the Albemarle region were
Paleo–Indian people who occupied the region more
than ten thousand years before the arrival of
Europeans and Africans.*

Murden-Brown House
111 West Queen Street
Late 1700s

Renovations to the house in 1988 revealed structural timbers dating from perhaps the late eighteenth century. Whether these timbers are the core of an earlier home or were reused lumber is unknown. Some believe an earlier structure was on this property prior to its purchase by Elisha Norfleet in 1795. Mr. Norfleet's will of 1807 refers to the property as the location of his office and garden.

Miss Eliza F. Mason, who rented the house, operated a girls' school here from the 1840s until the late 1850s. From 1859 until 1870, the property was owned by the Edenton Baptist Church and used as a parsonage. Charles M. Murden, an undertaker and proprietor of a saddlery, purchased the property for $325 in 1870, at which time there was no mention of buildings.

By 1895 there was a two story double-pile house similar to the existing dwelling. Miles G. Brown and his wife, Patsy Ann (Chappell) Brown acquired the house in 1922 as their personal residence. After the death of Mr. Brown, Mrs. Brown had the house remodeled by contractor Frank Fred Muth, who was an expert at remodeling older houses into the Colonial Revival style. This remodeling is evident today, particularly in the diminutive portico with its covered pediment supported by Doric pillars.

In 1944 the house was acquired by Ernest A. and Wilma C. Swain. Mr. Swain was principal of Edenton School, and when the new high school was built in the 1950s, the old school was renamed in his honor. The Swains resided here until 1988.

Bond-Lipsitz-Small House
112 West Queen Street
Unknown

Some local tradition claims this house dates from around 1790 although no elements from before the late nineteenth century remain visible. The present house, minus the tower bay on the east, appears on the 1893 Sanborn map, the earliest to date this block.

The house's ownership changed over the years: the Bond family from 1868–1899, the Haste family from 1899–1904, the Lipsitz from 1904–1915, and the Small family from 1948–1962.

The elaborately detailed Eastlake porch, added during the 1890s or early in the 1900s, displays a variety of turned, sawn, and drilled ornamentation. Mr. Lipsitz enlarged the house one bay on the east soon after 1910, adding the octagonal tower at the southeast. This tower and the corresponding clipped corner of the porch are unique among the many double-tier porches of Edenton.

The Edenton Tea Party is believed to be the first organized political action by women in the American Colonies.

Rea-Vail House
113 West Queen Street
Circa 1885

A fine example of a one-story Victorian cottage, this modestly scaled dwelling is decorated with an array of millwork that was added about ten years after the house's completion. The home was built for Willie D. Rea (1852–1902), the widow of Thomas D. Rea (1848–1884). Her son, W. D. Rea, was a co-owner of the Winborne and Rea Novelty Works, a local manufacturer of decorative Victorian woodwork. The firm was in operation only from the mid 1890s to 1900, a period that would coincide with the addition of the fancy elements to Mrs. Rea's porch.

On the rear of the house is the former detached kitchen, which was erected at the turn of the twentieth century and originally connected by an open porch. The double-pile interior features a spacious central hall that connects front and rear porches. The finish is simple with Colonial Revival mantels replacing the original Victorian fixtures.

In 1909, Rea's heirs sold the house to general store merchant Joseph Matthew Vail (1874–1959) and his wife Ruth (Newbold) Vail (1889–1956).

Skinner-Chappell House
116 West Queen Street
Mid-1890s

One of the few double-pile houses with double-tier porches in Edenton, this residence was built during the 1890s for grocer J. M. Skinner, who purchased this lot from Harding B. Perkins, a general merchant, in 1883.

The porch is enclosed by a balustrade of unusually intricate sawn slats. Of note is the distinctive coved entrance, recessed between elegantly concave walls sided with vertical tongue-and-groove boards. The interior contains well executed woodwork and beaded tongue-and-groove board wainscots.

Behind the house is an important early smokehouse, probably dating from the late eighteenth century. The door has a handsome nailing pattern. Whether this smokehouse dates from a previous house on this lot or was moved here later is uncertain. The current owners have stabilized the foundation of this structure.

Skinner sold the property in 1903 to Rufus Edward Chappell (1958–1931) and his wife, Sarah (Bond) Chappell. Mr. Chappell was a farmer who built numerous rental houses in Edenton.

Pruden-Goodwin House
118 West Queen Street
Circa 1922

John Henry Pruden purchased this lot in 1922, and Frank Fred Muth built the house that same year. The deep porch, triangular roof brackets, an exterior end half-shoulder chimney, and multiple pane-over-one sash windows are all traditional Bungalow elements. The interior has a modest Colonial Revival finish.

A native of Hertford County, Mr. Pruden was a conductor for the Norfolk Southern Railroad, coming to Edenton about 1919. There is no known relationship between John Henry Pruden and William D. Pruden, who came to Edenton from Hertford County in the early 1870s.

In 1930 Mr. Pruden and his wife, Mollie, moved to Norfolk and sold the house to Earl Goodwin, a grocery store proprietor, and his wife, Elizabeth (Holmes) Goodwin. In August 1956 they sold the house to their daughter and moved to the McDowell-Holmes House at 205 East Water Street.

Leigh-Hathaway House
120 West Queen Street
Circa 1759

An important early house in Edenton, the original gambrel roof dwelling here was erected between 1756 and 1759 by builder Gilbert Leigh, apparently as his own residence. The one-and-a-half story house is the oldest example of the side-passage double-pile house in Edenton. This house style would achieve considerable popularity during the late eighteenth and early nineteenth centuries.

The two-bay dwelling was enlarged in the 1820s with the addition of a two story section on the east. The porch was extended across both sections and updated with slender posts, molded capitals, round handrail, and slender rectangular-in-section balusters. As was traditional on Edenton houses built near the street, the steps were situated at each end of the porch.

The upstairs hall displays a painted floor of muted red and white checkerboard motif. Although the present floor is a repainted version of the original, it is a highly important illustration of decorative arts from the late eighteenth century. It has been copied by the Museum of Early Southern Decorative Arts in Winston-Salem for the floors of their Edenton Rooms.

Leigh-Bush House
166 West Queen Street
Circa 1759

The earliest section of this house, the single-pile side-hall plan block on the west, was erected between 1756 and 1759 by builder Gilbert Leigh. Little of the original house remains visible on the exterior, the dwelling having been enlarged and updated several times.

The house was enlarged into a center-hall plan, covered with a low hip roof, and given a two-story ell in the early nineteenth century. The double tier porch was added during the 1880s when the house was modernized into the Victorian style.

Gilbert Leigh was an active builder during the 1750s and 1760s in Edenton. After he sold the house at 120 West Queen Street, he probably resided here until 1771 when it was sold. In 1804 the house was purchased by Joseph and Ann Bozman, who probably undertook its expansion. In 1878 the house was acquired by Mrs. Elizabeth S. (Thompson) Bush, the wife of merchant Abram T. Bush.

William Scott Privott House
119 West Church Street
Between 1920 and 1927

After buying the lot in 1914, William Scott Privott moved the 1880 house to 117 West Church Street, where it remains, so he could construct a new home. According to the Sanborn maps, the home now displaying Colonial Revival symmetry was built between 1920 and 1927.

Privott's new house is sheltered beneath a hip roof that has broad boxed eves accented by pairs of elegantly curved brackets. The porch is carried by Tuscan columns, continuing with uncovered terraces to sunrooms on each side. A handsome wrought iron railing encloses the porch and accents the roof of each sunroom.

An attorney, Privott was a member of the North Carolina House of Representatives from 1909 to 1911.

William D. Pruden Sr. House
116 West Church Street
Circa 1883

This Italianate Victorian home was built for attorney William Dossey Pruden Sr. (1847–1918) on a lot acquired by his wife, Mary "Mollie" A.G. (Norfleet) Pruden (1847–1887). Pruden, a lawyer, was active in civic and political affairs, serving as Edenton's mayor during the late 1870s.

The original appearance of Pruden's home is unknown, except it was probably erected by contractor Theo Ralph. Evidence of the original exterior of the house has not been discovered, but there are ghost marks indicating changes made on some of the interior floors.

In the early twentieth century the house was substantially remodeled into its present form by contractor Frank Fred Muth. The eclectic combination of design elements results in a picturesque composition. Splendid coved eaves on the low hip roof provide an elegant transition between wall and roof. A second story sleeping porch on the East side provides a welcome retreat on a warm summer day.

Victorian interior elements have been maintained including plaster ceiling medallions, faux marble slate mantels, tiled fireplace hearths, and pocket doors between the living and dining areas. The whole picture has been set off by a Victorian iron fence, parts of which have recently been restored and duplicated by a local craftsman.

Leila Major White House
113 West Church Street
1920

George E. Major (1854–1933), the co-owner of Major and Loomis saw and planning mill in Hertford had this handsome Bungalow style residence erected in 1920 for his daughter, Leila (Major) White (1885–1957).

Sheltered beneath a slightly asymmetrical juxtaposition of broad gable roofs, the house features academic Bungalow elements, including slightly tapered brick porch pillars on the low railing wall, multi-pane sash windows, triangular brackets, slight battering of the gable's skirt and fine Craftsman lanterns at the entrance. It is the only Bungalow in town with an exterior-front chimney, a distinctive form of the style.

The rear has a second-story sleeping porch, added because of the early twentieth century belief that sleeping in unheated rooms was healthy, particularly as prevention against tuberculosis.

Folk–Taylor House
112 West Church Street
Circa 1899

The Queen Anne style house was built by George P. Folk soon after he bought the lot in 1899. The contractor was almost surely Theo Ralph. The modified L-plan house is dominated by the prominent front gable which shelters a small engaged porch on the second story. The interior follows the reception hall plan and is handsomely finished with Victorian and Colonial Revival style elements.

A native of Smithfield, Va., Folk came to Edenton as the cashier of the Bank of Edenton. In 1898, he married Caroline Gillian Wood (1877–1954), the daughter of Edward Wood Jr. In 1906, the Folks moved to Raleigh and sold their home to Samuel William Taylor (1874–1949). In 1925, Taylor and his wife, Ada Leona (Byrum) Taylor (1881–1964), opened the Taylor Theater, Edenton's first modern moving picture hall. The Taylors remained in this house until their deaths.

Edmund R. Conger House
110 West Church Street
1910

One of the most impressive Colonial Revival style houses in Edenton, this is the largest and most elaborate of a quartet of similar gambrel roof dwellings built by contractor Frank Fred Muth. The two-and-a-half story house focuses on the projecting second and third stories of the central bay, where a pedimented roof crowns a Palladian window on the second story and a tripartite window on the third story; Palladian motifs repeat on the gambrel ends. Stylish elements include extensive boxed eaves embellished with delicate swags and a deep wrap-around porch carried by paired Tuscan columns on paneled pedestals.

The center-hall plan interior has commodious dimensions and a sophisticated Colonial Revival finish. Perhaps the most outstanding element is the splendid east parlor mantel, comprised of large earthenware tiles in the design that is most remarkable for its simplicity.

The house was erected in 1910 by Edmund H. Conger (1857–1943), and his wife, Hattie (Gillingham) Conger (1861–1941). A native of Ohio, Conger came to Edenton from South Carolina and organized the Edenton Ice and Cold Storage Company, with a large plant on the water front.

C. S. Vann House
108 West Church Street
1910

Labeled on the 1910 Sanborn map as "Being Built," this handsome Colonial Revival style dwelling was the home of attorney Charles Spurgeon Vann (1857–1925) and his wife, Virginia (Pendelton) Vann (1869–1957). The Vann's had resided earlier at 205 East Water Street.

The house is covered by a pedimented roof and focuses on an extensive wrap-around porch of Tuscan columns. The small central second story porch shares a continuation of the fine boxed cornice that encircles the house.

The spaciousness of the interior is accented by over-scaled doors framed by wide Colonial Revival moldings. The handsome stairs, with a leaded glass window at the landing, suggests the work of Frank Fred Muth.

———————————

Robert B. Drane House
106 West Church Street
Circa 1897

Robert Brent Drane, D.D. (1851–1939) had this Queen Anne style dwelling erected as rental property sometime after his purchase of this lot in March 1897. The house, sheltered by a tall truncated pyramidal roof punctuated by gables, is similar to designs by Knoxville, Tennessee architect George F. Barber, who supplied plans for several Edenton dwellings during the late 1890s.

Enlivened by a front bay window, a small second story porch, elaborate window hoods, and wood shingled gables adorn the front of the house. The porch has replacement Colonial Revival pillars. The interior is spacious in plan but modest in finish, reflecting its rental purpose. Dr. Drane was the rector at St. Paul's Episcopal Church from 1876 to 1932, and lived in the rectory adjacent to the east.

St. John the Evangelist Episcopal Church, one of several
African-American congregations in Edenton was
organized around the time of the Civil War.

William M. Bond House
105 West Church Street
1893

This modest front gable home, along with the one next door at 107 West Church Street, was built as rental property by William M. and Laura G. Bond in 1893. An 1888 deed indicates the property was the former orchard of the Bonds, who lived down the street. The local newspaper regularly reported on the construction progress. Each house originally had a side-hall plan, a full-width front porch, and a two- room ell. This home was expanded with a two-story wing on the east and a wrap-around Colonial Revival porch.

In 1774, fifty-one Edenton women led by Penelope Barker protested the British king's taxation and staged their own "Edenton Tea Party" of sorts.

St. Paul's Episcopal Church Rectory
102 West Church Street
Circa 1897

This remodeled Queen Anne style house was erected about 1897 as a residence for the rector at St. Paul's Episcopal Church. The house originally had a porch that extended along the front and east elevations; the porch was largely reduced in size in the 1970s. The current home replaced an older rectory, as illustrated on the 1769 Sauthier map, the first rectory owned by the parish.

The rectory's first occupant was the family of the Rev. Robert Brent Drane, D.D. (1851–1939), and his wife Maria Lousia (Skinner) Warren Drane (1859–1921); Dr. Drane was the longest serving rector at St. Paul's from 1876 to 1932. This house continues to this day as the church's rectory.

Dr. Drane built the house at 106 West Church Street as a rental property.

St. Anne's Roman Catholic Church
209 North Broad Street
Circa 1858

One of nine Roman Catholic churches in North Carolina at the outbreak of the Civil War, it is the only one still in active use as a parish church. St. Anne's Church is a rare and handsome example of the antebellum Romanesque Revival style. The focus of the three-bay by four-bay structure is the central two-story bell tower with corner buttress and battlement parapet.

Even though the town had no more than a dozen Catholics in the spring of 1857, three young Edenton women spearheaded efforts to build the church. The foundation of St. Anne's Church was started in May 1857; the cornerstone was laid on the feast of St. Anne, July 26, 1857, and the church's dedication in July 1858.

The tiny mission flourished before the Civil War came to Edenton in 1862, forcing many of the members to flee. Federal troops likely quartered in the church and their horses were stabled in the basement. A small graveyard is located on the northeast side of the church, and recent soundings have revealed more than 70 people buried in unmarked graves.

In the years following the war, the church fell into disrepair from lack of use. Restorations in 1878 added the stained glass windows. By 1897 the church was again in a depilated condition. The Benedictine monk in charge appealed to Mother Katherine Drexel, now Saint Katherine Drexel. She sent the necessary funds to preserve the church. vthe renovated church was dedicated in 1898.

Samuel F. Williams House
102 West Gale Street
1908

This formal colonial Revival style house, reminiscent of the temple-form Greek Revival house, was built in 1908 for Samuel Ferebee Williams (1849–1923) and his wife, Mary (Pearce) Williams (1866–1913). Williams came to Edenton in 1902 as captain of the *John W. Garrett,* a 351 foot long steamship owned and operated by the Norfolk Suffolk Railroad as a railroad ferry between Edenton and Mackey's Ferry in Washington County.

Frank Fred Muth drew the plans and built the house. The impressive façade features a large semi-circular louvered vent. The equally handsome porch is carried by Tuscan columns. As was common in Muth houses, the spacious entrance hall features a colored glass window at the stair. Stylish Colonial Revival elements are employed throughout the house. Williams and his wife resided here until their deaths. The house continued to be lived in by family members. During the early 1990s the house was purchased and extensive renovations took place.

Gale Street Baptist Church
120 West Gale Street
1895

In 1895 a new Baptist congregation was formed to be known as the Gale Street Baptist Church. The members worshipped in the Masonic Hall near the fair ground until the church building was completed. Construction started on the Gothic Revival structure soon after the congregation purchased the property.

The focus of the building is the tall, slender, four-stage bell tower that evokes images of an Italian campanile. Gothic arched windows with colored Queen Anne sash illuminate the sanctuary. The rectangular apse has a trio of arched windows, the central one a double lancet.

Edenton was the home of Harriet Jacobs, author, abolitionist, and fugitive slave, whose memoirs "Incidents in the Life of a Slave Girl, Written by Herself" was published in 1861. This book brought attention to the plight of slaves.

Walter S. White House
201 North Granville Street
Circa 1912

A handsome example of the Colonial Revival style, this impressive house was erected between 1910 and 1915 for farmer Walter Stanley White and his wife, Annie. Frank Fred Muth constructed the house on land owned by White's father.

The large front pediment that covers the house, enclosing a stylish Palladian window, is echoed by pediments over side bay windows and on the porch; the porch's oblique corner pavilion is particularly distinctive.

In 1909, White, in support of his farming interest, became one of the largest investors in the incorporation of the Edenton Peanut Company.

Booth House
108 North Granville Street
Circa 1779

One of the three gambrel roof dwellings to survive in Edenton, this house was constructed in two stages during the eighteenth century at 133 East Church Street. The oldest section was built for Willis Williams soon after he inherited the lot from his father, Hatten Williams in 1779. The original one-room plan house consisted only of the western two bays.

Willis Williams was a sea captain, probably the same Willis Williams who was a commander of the *Caswell,* one of two galleys equipped in 1776 to guard Ocracoke Inlet from British attack.

Henry Flury bought the house in 1791 and soon undertook an expansion, adding the present hall and east room, creating a center-hall arrangement. The interior of the Flury's addition displays handsome transitional Georgian-Federal woodwork. Remnants of an early, if not original, blue paint survive near the upper stair landing.

After changing hands many times, Leland Greenleaf Plant and his wife, Pattie Louise (Moore) Plant bought it in 1941. The next year they moved it across town to its present location, placed it so that the façade no longer faced the street, and remolded, adding a brick appendage.

James N. Pruden Sr. House
105 North Granville Street
Circa 1901

Theo Ralph built this home in about 1901 for James Norfleet Pruden (1873–1921) and Penelope McMullan Pruden (1877–1967). Active in educational improvements, attorney Pruden served for eighteen years on the Board of Trustees of the Graded Schools. A plaque was placed on the Edenton Graded School in Pruden's honor, which reads, "A man of fine intellect, courteous manner and strong affection, he was unsurpassed in loyalty to pupils, teachers, and interests of the public school and the school public."

The home combines the asymmetry of the Queen Anne style with Colonial Revival finishes. A tall hip roof with a variety of gables and dormers dominates the roofline. The extensive porch, with plain Tuscan pillars, underscores the conservative Colonial-Revival style.

Around 1918, contractor Frank Fred Muth finished the upper story and remodeled the center-hall plan first floor. Original interior finishes combine Victorian moldings with Colonial Revival mantels, doors, stair, and a hall screen with fluted Doric pillars.

Bond-McMullan-Elliott House
200 West Church Street
1860

This imposing house results from a circa 1891 expansion of an antebellum house and a early twentieth century remodeling. The original home was built for merchant Alexander H. Bond (born circa 1831) and his wife Sarah R. (Simpson) Bond (circa 1834–1894). Bond purchased two lots here in August 1860 from Baker White for $250, and construction commenced shortly thereafter. The original two-and-a-half story, side-hall plan, double-pile house consisted of the present hall and eastern tier of rooms.

In 1890, Mrs. Bond sold the house, and it was acquired the next year by Dr. John Henry McMullan. He and his wife Lina enlarged the house to a center hall plan by adding a two-story double-pile block on the west. The house was given a Victorian finish with an elaborately decorated porch.

After the deaths of the McMullans, the property was inherited by their daughter, Mildred (1885–1974), the wife of Oscar Moore Elliott (1885–1960), a retail clothier. They then transformed the house into the Colonial Revival style.

Most of the exterior, including the imposing two-story pillars, dates from the Colonial Revival remodeling of Frank Fred Muth, a builder capable of replicating nineteenth century architectural elements. The trabeated entrance remains framed by Greek-Revival moldings.

Rea-Miller House
202 West Church Street
Circa 1894

Erected for fisherman J. K. Rea after he purchased this lot in May 1894, this house features a variation of the double-tier porch. The porches and house are simply finished, including semi-circular louvered gable vents. The Victorian hairpin fence was moved from the Louis F. Ziegler House, the North Carolina State Historic State. The interior features Victorian elements and Eastlake mantels.

In 1942, John Frank Miller, a Bertie County farmer and the operator of a hardware store on Broad Street, acquired the property where he and his wife lived until their deaths in the late 1950s.

A two story addition was added to the rear of the house in the 1980s. At that time the main level and the second level of the original house were converted to two apartments.

The Roanoke River Lighthouse has survived over 129 years despite hurricanes, floods, war, neglect, ice floes, and three moves.

116

Baker-White House
204 West Church Street
Circa 1855

This house was built for Baker White who acquired four lots here in 1855 for $225. The house remained in the Baker White family until 1891.

This simple one story frame dwelling is a notable example of the "coastal cottage" popular throughout coastal North Carolina during the eighteenth and early nineteenth centuries. The style is defined by a broad gable roof, here without the commonly seen double-pitch slope that engages a full width porch. As this house type was usually associated with modestly scaled dwellings, stylish character was typically subdued, as here reflected by the austere Greek-Revival elements.

While the porch pillars are replacements, the original pilasters at each corner display simple molded Greek-Revival bases and capitals. Of note is the plain bottom board that continues around the house. Completing the house are symmetrical surrounds with corner blocks and exterior-end brick chimneys. On the rear center is an originally detached two-room kitchen, its porch being supported by tapered pillars on short pedestals.

The center hall plan interior has a straight forward Greek-Revival finish with simple moldings, two paneled doors, and attractive pilaster-and-frieze form mantles with peaked backboards. In the kitchen a six paneled Federal style door with delicate molded surround suggests that the kitchen may be somewhat older than the house.

Paine House
100 South Granville Street
Circa 1844

An important regional example of the coastal cottage form, this commodious one-and-a-half story dwelling was built for Colonel Robert T. Paine, probably soon after his purchase of this lot in 1844. Displaying the form's characteristic broad double-slope gable roof with a deep engaged front porch, the house is finished in the prevailing Greek-Revival style. The porch is carried by Doric pillars and enclosed by a fine swan slat railing.

A handsome but austere trabeated entrance leads to a spacious center hall that continues throughout the house to the rear ell. The focus is on a novel Tudor Revival arch that spans the hall, dividing the front hall from the rear hall, where the modestly scaled stair is located. The arch provides a striking, almost whimsical, contrast to the otherwise austere Greek-Revival interior.

---

*Edenton resident Hugh Wiliamson was a
signer of the United State Constitution.*

Twine-Satterfield House
104 South Granville Street
Circa 1904

William E. Twine had this pleasant Victorian dwelling erected soon after he purchased this lot November 1904. The design focuses on a wood shingled front pediment and a large porch with handsome Colonial-Revival replacement pillars.

The porch was modernized for farmer John Thomas Satterfield (1862–1933) and his wife, Lurinda (Sutton) Satterfield (1869–1960), after they bought the house in 1906. Frank Fred Muth, who built or remodeled many Edenton homes, was the contractor. Interior modifications include the rearrangement of hall and south parlor to form an entrance foyer, a plan Muth favored. The Satterfields were succeeded in the house first by their son, Cliff Satterfield, and then their daughter, Celia Satterfield (1901–1985).

Blount Street was at one time a five-track railroad yard with a lumber mill.

Dr. Henry M. S. Cason House
108 South Granville Street
Circa 1907

An imposing example of the Neo-Classical Revival style, this house was built in 1907 for Dr. Henry Marchand Shaw Cason (1878–1924) and his wife, Alice (Makely) Cason (1880–1924). Frank Fred Muth was the contractor, and family tradition holds that he and Mrs. Cason drew up the plans.

The house is dominated by a monumental two-story portico with paired Tuscan columns supporting the balustrade roof. Pedimented dormers, dentiled modillion cornices, and large one-over-one sash windows further distinguish the house. Stained glass windows, a Muth trademark, are used to flank the foyer's impressive Adamesque-Revival mantel.

A native of Edenton, Cason at first maintained his doctor's office in the rear of the house, but this was not satisfactory and he moved his offices on East King Street. Cason also dabbled in the automobile business, ordering Fords for himself and his friends and later getting the necessary replacement parts.

In 1910s, he built a showroom and repair garage behind his mother's house at the northeast corner of Broad and Queen Street. In 1918, he enlarged his garage so that he could have his Ford and medical practice together, and by the time of his death he had all but given up medicine in favor of the automobile business.

In 1989–1990, the house was renovated for a bed-and-breakfast inn.

Goodwin-Leggett House
205 South Granville Street
Circa 1884

The impressive brick residence, erected about 1884, is the finest Italianate style house in Edenton. Italianate elements include asymmetrical massing, low hip roof, bracketed boxed cornice, rusticated quoins, boxed window hoods with sawn detailing, and sturdy chamfered porch pillars. The spacious center-hall plan interior was well appointed in the fashion of the 1880s.

The house's early history is associated with industrialists who, perhaps, chose the house as a reflection of their own ambitions. The home's first owner, Silas W. Goodwin, was the proprietor of a grist and saw mill in Edenton. The next owner was the superintendent of the Pease Lumber Company. The third owner was also in the grist and lumber business.

Walter Augustus Leggett (1872–1950), a local druggist, purchased the house in 1905. The house and tin roof were painted dark red, with each brick outlined by white "penciling." In 1923, Leggett and his wife, Jessie (Herman) Leggett (1875–1949) undertook a renovation of the house, which included re-painting the exteriors but excluded the labor intensive penciling.

Edenton Baptist Church
206 South Granville Street
1916–1920

The third building erected by Edenton Baptists, this impressive Colonial Revival style edifice was designed by Charlotte architect J.M. McMichael, one of the state's leading designers of churches. While the cornerstone was laid in 1916, World War I slowed the church's completion and dedication was held in 1920. The design is dominated by a copper-covered dome resting on an octagonal base. The dramatic dome, with its oculus window filled with vibrant colored glass, commands the impressive Colonial-Revival sanctuary.

The Edenton Baptist Church was organized in 1817 and its first building burned in 1870. It was replaced by a Gothic Revival structure which was demolished after completion of the new church in 1916.

Although it has been inactive since 1942, a small cemetery remains on the property. At least twelve graves stones date before the Civil War. Although none of the gravestones remaining in the section of the cemetery are marked with the name of the stone carver, several are handsome examples of funerary symbolism. Certainly the most evocative is the little angel with downcast eyes.

Index

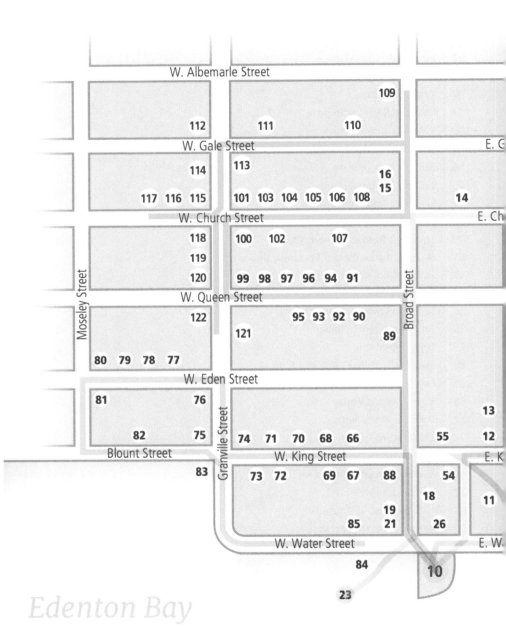

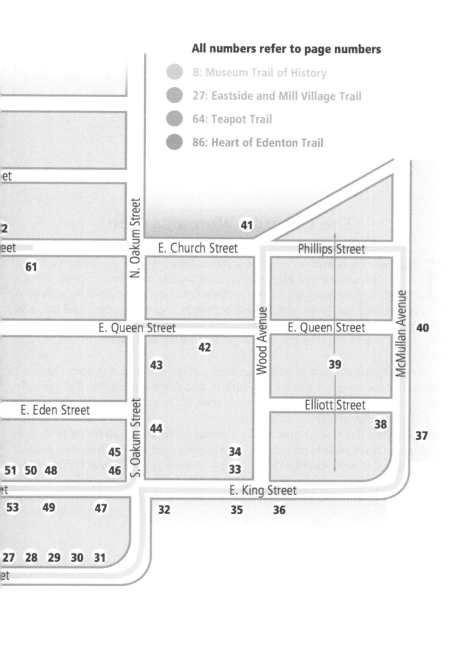

All numbers refer to page numbers

- 8: Museum Trail of History
- 27: Eastside and Mill Village Trail
- 64: Teapot Trail
- 86: Heart of Edenton Trail

The Edenton Woman's Club

The Edenton Woman's Club (EWC) started life in 1946 as the Junior Woman's Club, becoming the Edenton Woman's Club in 1951. Its chief service focus is the preservation and restoration of historic Edenton, with continuing support for Town of Edenton activities and endeavors. The biennial Edenton Pilgrimage, held since 1949, is the major fundraiser for the Club's service projects and enables the organization to help in a variety of restoration projects.

As additional support of historical preservation, the Club has commissioned two books focusing on historical Edenton and Chowan County: *Between the River and the Sound: The Architectural Heritage of Chowan County, North Carolina* and *Edenton: An Architectural Portrait*.

Antiquities has twice honored the Edenton Woman's Club for its preservation work. Other awards include the C. H. Verner Cup, Halifax Resolves Award, Gertrude S. Caraway Award of Merit, and Andrew J. Howell Silver Tray Award.